THE GAMES INDIA PLAYS

THE GAMES INDIA PLAYS

Indian Sports Simplified

Amitabh Satyam
Sangeeta Goswami

BLOOMSBURY
NEW DELHI • LONDON • OXFORD • NEW YORK • SYDNEY

BLOOMSBURY INDIA
Bloomsbury Publishing India Pvt. Ltd
Second Floor, LSC Building No. 4, DDA Complex, Pocket C – 6 & 7,
Vasant Kunj, New Delhi 110070

BLOOMSBURY, BLOOMSBURY INDIA and the Diana logo
are trademarks of Bloomsbury Publishing Plc

First published in India 2022
This edition published 2022

ISBN: PB: 978-93-54351-64-8; e-Book: 978-93-54352-56-0
2 4 6 8 10 9 7 5 3 1

Typeset in Fournier MT Std by Manipal Technologies Limited
Printed and bound in India by Thomson Press India Ltd.

MIX
Paper from responsible sources
FSC® C010615

CONTENTS

LIST OF FIGURES

ACKNOWLEDGEMENTS

We express our gratitude to the publishers at Bloomsbury, Praveen Tiwari and Nitin Valecha, for their extraordinary partnership and support.

We also thank Shreya Nand Shah for her support in developing the drawings.

NAVIGATING THE BOOK

Chapter 1 introduces the context of Indian games and their disappearance over the last 50 to 100 years. We also discuss the qualities of an interesting game and the ways games improve our physical, mental and emotional well-being. Towards the end of this chapter, we provide an outline of the structure of the chapters describing each game.

From Chapter 2 to Chapter 16, we cover 15 games in detail. We have presented these games in no particular order.

In Chapter 17, we have included 14 games with short descriptions as worthy mentions.

The last chapter highlights the specific benefits of playing these games. We also establish the connection of these games to our ancient culture and assert that preserving these indigenous games is akin to preserving our culture.

1

Let the Games Begin

India's sports culture is thousands of years old, with countless games developed and played in the region. These games, however, are not popular in urban India today. As the British lived in cities and towns,[1] these regions converted to playing British games first. When urban Indians think of sports, we think of cricket, hockey, tennis, badminton, squash, golf, football, volleyball, basketball, table tennis, billiards and carom—all Western sports. Indigenous games have been eliminated from the active consideration of Indians.

Schools and colleges organise competitions for these Western sports only, and social and sports clubs also have facilities for only these sports. Indian sports, such as kabaddi, *lagori*, *gutte*, *nondi* and hundreds of others, have slowly disappeared. Medals won and success in sports, in general, are measured only by performance in these Western sports. Accordingly, when there is talk of investing in sports in India, only the development of Western sports facilities, such as cricket stadiums and tennis courts, is considered, ignoring traditional sports. Kabaddi has been revived as a TV show, but we do not

[1] In other words, the places where the British (or earlier rulers) lived became prominent cities.

see it played in apartment complexes. Indian games are not played in CBSE/ICSE schools, missionary schools or English-medium schools. Even vernacular-medium state-run schools have moved away from playing Indian games, probably because Western games are positioned as cool and aspirational.

Indian games are immensely exciting, as is evident from their lasting presence over thousands of years. Like the sustained sidelining of Indian languages, these games have also been actively neglected in favour of foreign games. Children in villages and small towns still play a few of these games, but the frequency and coverage are dwindling as Western games are promoted on TV with aspirational value. Even in villages, informal cricket grounds have come up.

> With colonisation, local cultures were decimated substantially, and the games played by the colonisers became the mainstream in most of these countries.

Our endeavour in this book is to pick a few popular games and present them in a convenient format for use as a guidebook for playing. This book covers all information needed to play, including methods, equipment required, ground design, team configurations, rules and strategies. To maintain the focus on playability, the book provides no extra information.

Just like food, clothing and languages, games also grow out of the region's topography, climate and available natural resources. Games are, consequently, unique to a region, and over millennia, thousands of games have been developed all over the world. Therefore, games in India, Africa and Canada will, expectedly, be different. However, with colonisation, local cultures were destroyed by and large, and games played by the colonisers became mainstream in most of these countries.

A few components—for example, sticks and balls—are similar in games across the world. Most equipment-based games are derived from these two elements, which are operated using hands and feet. Many games, in particular, Indian games, do not use any equipment; they are based on the configuration of players and their movement and on the types of constraints applied when playing.

The games in this book

After extensive research, we have selected 15 games for detailed illustration in this book. As expected, traditional games were played in open fields with basic or no equipment. Tournaments were also held, and there were set rules for each game. Even so, most of these games can also be played impromptu without any planning.

The games presented have the following features:

1. They have a detailed set of rules for each step during the game.
2. They have many variations that allow possibilities to develop while playing, thus inviting players to innovate.

3. These are fun to play with a large number of possible outcomes, maximising the involvement of each player at all times during the play. These games have no or little downtime for any players, as opposed to, for example, cricket. In cricket, only two players are the most active, namely the batsman and the bowler.

Without insistence on adherence to the rules, no game is interesting.

4. The games can be played with no or minimal equipment. Equipment, if any, costs only a little or can be prepared locally by the players. For example, players can make *gilli danda* sticks by shaping thin branches of trees from their neighbourhood.
5. They can be played without any planning. A few friends can decide to play many of these games impromptu.
6. They have established rules; some can be customised or relaxed depending on the field, the number of players and the equipment available. But the rules must be followed. Without adherence to the rules, no game is interesting.
7. The playing field is well-defined. Nevertheless, in most cases, any open area can be used. Unlike tennis or squash, the excitement of these games is embedded in the format and not necessarily dependent on the configuration of the field. Many of these games are played on streets. However, considering today's traffic in cities, the players must assess the availability of such spaces for playing.

8. Except a few, all are group games with team dynamics at play, promoting camaraderie and competition.

Sports versus games

The terms 'sports' and 'games' are often used synonymously. Let us understand these terms to facilitate our narrative.

Sports is a generic term used to describe physical activities, whereas games have a goal to achieve using physical and mental faculties. Sports include non-competitive activities, such as running, hiking, swimming and exercising, whereas games need at least one opponent to compete with. Games have a scoring system with a win-lose decision at the end. Therefore, chess, ludo and Monopoly are games with specific sets of skills involved, and, in each game, there are specific sets of rules and strategies. These games would not be classified as sports.

> Just like the case of our education system, once the British came, Indians stopped playing Indian games, and British games became our games too.

Sports measure individual prowess, such as muscular strength, agility and swiftness. The player can make decisions independently to perform better or worse. In a game, in addition to physical prowess and mental competence, players have to respond to the opponent's actions and coordinate with the team members.

Why do we enjoy playing games?

Games are an enjoyable form of recreation and entertainment for a player. Engaging in intense physical exercise releases neurotransmitters—dopamine, the happy hormone, and norepinephrine, which works as an antidepressant. They trigger euphoric feelings, provide happiness, enhance moods, elevate energy levels and improve memory recall.

You would have observed that people who engage in intense physical activity have high energy levels all the time. They get tired less frequently compared to those who do not do much physical work.

In summary, players love games due to the following reasons:

1. The endorphins released due to physical activity give a natural high. Endorphins are designed to help survival from a biological perspective and provide a feeling of well-being.[2]
2. Games take the players to a new world with new experiences. Nature has made us all explorers, and we are designed to enjoy new experiences.
3. Well-designed games, just like the ones covered in this book, have many variations and possibilities, giving the player a sense of newness. The unpredictable nature of the next steps keeps them engaged.

> Do you know what my favourite part of the game is? The opportunity to play.
>
> —Mike Singletary

[2] https://www.nature.com/articles/npp2017148

4. During the play, the players are deeply engrossed in the game, ported to a new world. It takes them away from the stresses of day-to-day life, such as examination preparation, poor performance at work, relationship conflicts or marital distress.
5. Players feel a sense of achievement and self-validation. When a player does well, the great shot or great tactic is remembered for a long time and often keeps playing in the mind, positively reinforcing the player's ego.
6. Even losing makes the players think about the reasons for the loss and plans to do better the next time. It adds to new experiences and training of the mind.
7. Novelty, the unpredictability of situations and changes in the configurations make the players constantly devise new ways of addressing the situation to win.
8. Flexibility and varied strategies stimulate creativity. The best players are also the most creative; creativity needs refinement of instincts and mental alertness.

What is a game?

A series of activities cannot be called a game. Inherent to a game is the setting of the objectives, the performance of a series of activities to achieve those objectives and a set of well-defined constraints against which the activities have to be performed. In addition, these activities require skills beyond those needed for day-to-day routine tasks. Here, we present the key characteristics of an interesting game.

Defined objectives

Each game has a well-defined objective for each role of the players as well as for the whole game. An interesting game requires skills, activities, unpredictable events, instantaneous coordination, directed response and defined outcomes. For example, hitting the ball to the boundary to gain four points in cricket is a defined objective. Similarly, touching the defenders to gain a point is defined as an objective in kabaddi, as is scoring goals in football. Defined objectives drive players to devise strategies to achieve those objectives.

Constraints

Constraints are the restrictions applied to the players either as rules or boundaries. These constraints make the game interesting as the players have to strategise each move to choose a path that takes them to their objectives, but within these constraints. These constraints include the opponent's moves and their positions, time constraints, boundaries drawn, and positions of physical objects. For example, in kabaddi, we have the constraints of the breathing time limit and boundary lines. The opposing team restricts freedom, and the objective is to overcome these limitations triumphantly and eliminate many members of the opposing team from the game. Similarly, the defending team is limited by the boundary line. In cricket, the objective is to hit the ball as far as it can go unobstructed, and the constraint is the strategically positioned fielders. The skill is in interpreting the ball movement and hitting within these constraints. In tennis and badminton, there are boundary lines and the readiness of the opposing player at a spot on the court.

Without these constraints, the game will cease to be exciting. Imagine no single breath time constraint or drawn lines in kabaddi. Each game must have a way to conclude each move within a reasonable time and space limit.

Individual initiative and decision-making

> Game = {unpredictable events, instantaneous coordination, directed response and defined outcomes}

Each player in an exciting game is always busy either actively executing a task or strategising. For instance, in kabaddi, the raiders actively optimise the time left in their breath and look for any weakness in the defending team that they can take advantage of without getting caught. Members of the defending team are on their toes and actively pursue the raider. The members of the raider team, while watching for a minute or so, observe the ongoing play and strategise who should raid next based on the current situation. Volleyball, basketball and tennis are gripping games, as each player has an active role during the entire period of the game and must constantly analyse the situation and instantly act.

From that perspective cricket is not an interesting game for the players since half the team is waiting and watching—the batting team in the pavilion has practically no active role. They watch the game just like spectators. The captain and the coach strategise but not the players. Similarly, the fielders go into action only when the ball is bowled, and till then, they just stand. After the ball is played, only two or three players chase the ball; the rest still watch. Ludo also has a limited set of strategies and, therefore, is not exciting for many. Video games are designed to provide multiple possibilities to the players at crucial stages in the game. The games that allow for more possibilities more frequently make the game fascinating.

Defined reward

> An interesting game must have no activity that is not related to a reward or punishment, leading to a win or loss.

Each decision and its execution are connected to a reward-punishment system, as an award of points, win or expulsion. Each action by the player influences the success of the individual and the team. An interesting game must have no activity that is not related to a reward or penalty, leading to a win or a loss. In football, each good kick improves the chances of getting a goal, and a bad kick leads to a reduced chance of winning a goal and an increased possibility of the opposing team winning a goal.

Uncertainty and unexpected situations

Interesting games have situations that cannot be predicted far ahead. The unpredictability makes the game thrilling and dynamic, where each player responds to the new configurations. A snapshot of a game taken now and seconds later will find the players doing different things at different locations. A new situation develops during the game, and players must respond to move towards winning. For example, in tennis, one does not know exactly where the service ball will fall, and in a fraction of a second, the receiver of the service must react and hit a shot strategically, such that the opponent finds it hard to reach. In kabaddi, each movement of the raiders makes the entire defending team respond within a fraction of a second to save themselves and, at the same time, coordinate among themselves to attack the raider.

Unique skills applied

Each game requires a unique set of skills to succeed: some need quick response, some need precision and some need accuracy of judgement of a movement. A quick response is generally a universal need. In cricket, for the batting person, the ability to manoeuvre the bat to hit the ball as far as it can go without getting caught by the fielders is a unique skill. The same skill is not relevant in football. Cricket bowlers, similarly, must throw the ball to maximise the chances of the batting person getting out. In kabaddi, swift action and breath-holding power are required skills, along with physical strength. In squash, the ability to move laterally and quickly return to the middle of the court is a unique skill. Manoeuvring the ball with your feet without using your hands is a special skill needed for football.

Navigating the book

The architecture of the book is simple. After this introductory chapter, we have one chapter each for the games. Inside each chapter, we have sections describing the game's key components, such as the equipment, field dimensions and strategies, as described below.

Name of the game

We picked the most popular name in India as the chapter's name, and underneath, we mention other popular names used in different regions. The list of names given is not exhaustive as the same game may be known by another name in other regions. Inside the chapter, we have mentioned the names we researched along with the regions.

> There are children playing in the streets who could solve some of my top problems in physics, because they have modes of sensory perception that I lost long ago.
> —J. Robert Oppenheimer

Introduction

We present an overview of the game.

Other names

Here, we mention all the names of the game and their corresponding regions. Depending on the region you are from, the name that the game is popularly called in your region would be found there.

The play

This section covers all the aspects of the game during the play including:

1. the number of players on each side of the game, along with the minimum and the maximum number of players required to play without changing the game's structure;
2. equipment needed to play, including the size, shape, material and possibilities;
3. ground dimensions, positions of players at the beginning of the game and examples of the positions of the players during the game;
4. skills required to play the game, such as physical agility, strength and mental skills and
5. playing method described in detail with each player's roles, placement at each stage of the game and movements.

Scoring

Methods of scoring, counting of points, identification of good and bad moves, and addition and subtraction of points are covered in this section.

Rules

Rules mentioned here define the key framework and principles of the game and set the boundaries. These rules also help referees observe the players and judge compliance with the principles of the game. We have deliberately not delved too deep into the rules as we wish to allow the player to customise depending on the situation. The basic framework described here is adequate to play and enjoy the game.

Positions, tasks and techniques

Every game has a key set of strategies for winning. Prescribing these strategies can only help with basic levels of the game; good players evolve their own set of strategies and tricks. We stick to the basics to get you started, hoping you will build on it.

Key skills required

The games we selected can be played by any person of any age and gender. However, as the physical and mental strengths needed are different for each of these games, we highlight the unique set of skills needed to succeed, and not any gender or age.

Caution

Physical games require interaction with other moving players and moving objects. Each player responds to these movements as a part of playing the game and also needs to protect from these momentum-carrying objects. Standing at the wrong place, not moving fast enough, or inability to control one's movement leading to a collision with another player or an object, such as a wall, can cause injury. Sports injuries are common, and in this section, we highlight the risks and ways to prevent injuries.

Skills developed

Each game requires a specific set of strengths. Playing enhances some existing skills and develops some others. In this section, we highlight the physical and mental skill areas developed.

Teachers and guardians of children can use this section to find support for introducing one or more of these games in schools or their communities.

Life lessons

Playing games, teaches us lessons that touch our lives. In this section, we highlight the values these games bring to our lives.

The current state of the game

A few games, such as kabaddi and kho-kho are popular, and kabaddi has been revived after the formation of the sports league. We describe the current status and popularity of each game.

Variations of the game

Considering the long history of these games, many variations have evolved over time—some in the same region and many in other regions. We mention these variations briefly, highlighting any distinguishing features.

Similar games

Names of the games around the world which involve similar skills are given in this section.

Glossary

Definition and description of keywords used in the game are given.

The measurement units

We use both metres and feet for distance. Many games have been designed using the older foot-pound-second (FPS) system and many with the newer International System of Units (SI) that uses metres. We have left the round figures of the original; if we convert to SI only or FPS only, we will get decimal points that would be even less friendly.

2

Lagori

सतोलिया

નાગોલચુ

लिंगोरचा

ஏழு கல்

ഡബ്ബ കളി

ఏడు రాళ్ళు

সাতচারা

Seven stones

Introduction

Lagori is an outdoor team sport of using a ball to hit and break a stack of stone discs. After hitting the lagori or the stack of stone discs, the members of the breaker team rearrange the stack hurriedly while the opposing team catches the ball to quickly hit the breakers before the lagori is restacked. This game is founded on swift actions and well-timed responses.

Originating in southern India, the game is now popular all over the country and in many parts of the world, covering about 30 countries. The International

Lagori Federation governs the global community, sets rules and organises tournaments.

The name *satoliya* is equally popular in many parts of India, referring to the seven stone discs that are stacked.

Other names

TABLE 2.1

Region	*Name*	*Region*	*Name*
Maharashtra	*Lingorcha*	Andhra Pradesh	*Dikori, yedu rallu yedupenkulata*
Haryana, Punjab	*Pitthu garam*	Gujarat	*Nagolachu, satoliyu*
Rajasthan	*Sitoliya, pitthu phod, pittu garam*	Tamil Nadu	*Ezhu kallu, sachakal silli*
Bihar	*Sitoliya, pitto*	Kashmir	*Garman*
West Bengal	*Pittu*	Kerala	*Dabba kali, chatti panth, chattikali*
Canada	*Teelo*	Bangladesh	*Satchara*
Turkey	*Seven tiles*	Iran, Saudi Arabia	*Haft sang*
Bhutan, Uganda	*Seven stones*	Afghanistan	*Santacon*

The play

Lagori is played between two teams: breakers and defenders. Seven flat discs of varying sizes are stacked in the decreasing order of size, and the goal of the breakers is to knock over the stack with a throw of the ball. They must then collectively restore it quickly before the defenders can collect the ball and tag any team member.

The objective of the defending team is to strike any breaker with a throw of the ball, targeting below the knee level. If the ball touches any of the breakers, then that player and the entire team is declared out.

The ball then goes to the opposing team, and the next game begins with the defenders now as breakers.

Number of players

There are two teams with six players each in formal tournaments. The game can also be played with only two players on each side. While the game is more fun with more players, we do not recommend more than seven members in each team.

Equipment needed

1. One ball, soft enough not to cause any injury upon impact, is needed. A common rubber ball is adequate. Tennis balls are not recommended but are often used. Cricket or hockey balls are too hard to use.
2. Seven discs of different sizes are required, so they can be stacked in decreasing order of size. Flat earth tiles used for roofing are readily available and commonly used. Floor tiles are suitable as well. Most of the discs used for informal games do not have any specific form or size—they are just broken pieces that can stand as a stack.

3. Professional tournaments held under the aegis of the International Lagori Federation use nine fibre discs of standard sizes.

The playground

Lagori playgrounds can be set on grass fields, sand, concrete or any open area in an informal setting. A fixed boundary is not necessary, but the players must always be in the sight of all the other players and within reach of a ball throw.

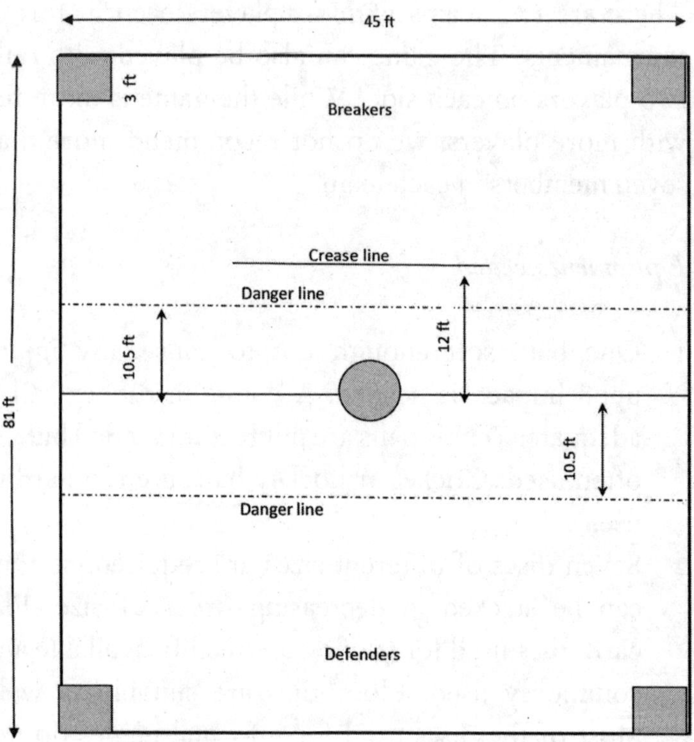

FIG. 2.1. The playground for lagori

For formal tournaments, the size of the playground is specified as follows:

1. Length = 81 ft, breadth = 45 ft
2. There are four boxes in the four corners of the rectangular court measuring 3 ft x 3 ft. We can ignore this for a casual game.
3. A centre line is drawn that divides the rectangular court into two equal parts.
4. A small circle is drawn in the middle of the centreline in which the discs are stacked to make lagori.
5. A line known as the danger line is drawn on either side of the centreline at a distance of 10.5 ft. Players from both sides must stand beyond this line.
6. The striker from the breakers' team stands behind the crease line, which is 12 ft from the centre line.

FIG. 2.2. Configuration of the field just before the hit

Players shown in black are the breakers, and the star inside the image depicts a breaker on strike.

FIG. 2.3. Configuration of the field just after the hit

Playing method

Set boundaries for the playing field. Draw a circle in the centre in which the seven stones are stacked on top of one another, with the smallest on the top to make a lagori (stack).

1. The striker team is called breakers, and the fielding team is known as defenders. A coin is tossed to choose which team will play the breakers' role first.
2. After the selection, the stones are stacked to form the lagori. Any of the defenders can do this. The discs are stacked to provide maximum stability and resistance to soft hits by a ball.
3. One of the defenders takes a position behind the stack at a distance of about 4 ft to catch the ball thrown by the striker. To catch the ball from any direction, other players will take positions by scattering around the lagori.
4. All the breakers will take their position behind the crease line in the breakers' part of the field.

5. One of the breakers, generally the one considered the best at aiming, starts the game by attempting to strike the lagori with a ball-throw from the crease line.
6. If the lagori is not disrupted and any defender catches the ball after the first bounce, then the striker will be declared out, and the next player of the breakers comes on the strike.
7. If the lagori is not disrupted and the defenders do not catch the ball, then the striker will get two more chances to knock over the stack. After three failed trials, that striker's turn is over, and the next player from the breakers will play.
8. The breakers get nine chances in total—three chances each for three players—to break the lagori.
9. After the lagori is broken, the defending players catch the ball and aim at the breakers to hit them below their knees or on their back.
10. At the same time, the breakers gather near the lagori and try to quickly restack the discs. They must stay alert to scatter rapidly because the defenders keep throwing the ball at them. The striker and rebuilders coordinate while dodging the ball thrown at them. This task is not easy because a member of the defending team stands near the lagori, waiting to get the ball from a teammate.
11. After restacking the lagori, the breakers trace a circle around it three times with their fingers and then shout 'lagori'. Thus, they get one point and also the chance to hit the stack again.
12. However, if the defenders succeed in hitting any breaker before they rebuild and shout lagori, then the breaker team is out. The ball will then go to the

defenders, and in the next game, they will be the breakers.

13. When the defenders get the ball to hit the breakers, they must not run with the ball. Instead, the player with the ball must throw it either directly at the breakers or to a teammate who has better chances of aiming at the breakers.
14. When the ball changes hands, the defenders play as the breakers.

Scoring

1. If breakers can rearrange the discs before getting tagged out, they get one point and the next turn to play as breakers.
2. If the defenders hit any of the breakers before restacking the lagori, the breakers would be out. The defenders get to play as breakers next. Defenders do not score any points for this.
3. The team that scores seven points first will be the winner.

Rules

1. If a striker cannot knock down the stack, then he or she is given two more chances—a total of three strikes. After three failed strikes, the ball goes to another team member.
2. If the breakers cannot knock down the lagori in nine tries, then the defenders get one point and will now get a turn to be the breakers.

3. In any of the three tries, if the striker's ball does not disrupt the stack and is caught by an opponent after one bounce (a tip) behind the lagori, then the striker is out.
4. Players from the defending team cannot run with a ball in their hand. The ball should not remain in the player's hands for more than 3 seconds. They have to keep passing the ball to their teammates who can tag breakers conveniently.

Position, tasks and techniques

TABLE 2.2

Roles	*Positions*	*Tasks*	*Strategy / Techniques*
Striker	Stand with a ball, just behind the crease line in alignment with lagori, ready to hit.	Aim at the lagori to knock it down with a ball throw. Join the other team members to restack the lagori immediately after knocking it down. Dodge the hit of the ball thrown by the defenders.	Try to knock over only one or two top discs of the lagori with a superficial hit to make it easier to restack rapidly. If the discs scatter to far places with a powerful direct hit, then it would take longer to collect and rebuild the lagori. The risk of a slow hit is that the ball stays close to the stack, increasing the chances of the opposing team hitting the breakers.

Roles	*Positions*	*Tasks*	*Strategy | Techniques*
Breakers, other than the striker	Stand beyond the crease line, behind the striker.	Wait for the lagori to be disrupted and rush to rebuild it quickly once it is broken.	First, focus on the actions and body language of the striker. Team up to rapidly rebuild the lagori. At the same time, keep observing the moves of the defenders to avoid getting tagged out with the ball thrown by them.
Defenders	Take positions as fielders, covering the entire ground, and prepare to catch the ball thrown by the striker.	First, stack the lagori. After the striker throws the ball, try to catch the ball. Tag any of the opponents with a ball throw after the lagori is broken.	Be vigilant about all the moves on the playfield and keep passing the ball to the teammates nearest to the re-stackers. Keep the ball moving to divert the attention of the breakers to impede the rebuilding of the lagori.

Key skills required

The players have to aim, throw, catch and run. These activities require skills in hand-eye coordination. Defenders must be swift to dodge a ball, and breakers should have steady hands and concentration to pile the discs quickly.

Individuals with no specific training but a reasonable fitness level that allows them to run a little and aim the players with a ball-throw can play this game. Children from ages six to eighteen years are most likely to be interested. The uniqueness of this game is that all the roles are situational and not fixed.

Caution

1. To avoid injuries, do not use a hard ball like a tennis ball.
2. Defenders should stand at an appropriate distance from the stack to save themselves from a direct hit while the striker targets the stack.

Skills developed

Lagori focuses on improving aiming precision, observation and swiftness simultaneously and enhances the ability to concentrate. It also enables physical exercises of running, catching and throwing. In addition, it helps develop teamwork and inculcates team spirit.

This fast-paced game has no role of a captain; no player has a fixed role. Everyone is involved at all times, and every player gets an opportunity to play, where they perform according to their abilities of decision-making, swiftness and deception.

Life lessons

1. *Leadership and coordination*: This game helps develop leadership and on-the-fly coordination of an unorganised group.
2. *Lessons for readjustment*: The game starts when the stone stack is destroyed and reassembled quickly. Players learn to rebuild when things fail or go wrong.
3. *Teamwork for winning:* The performance of each member of the team determines win or loss. Strong players can overcome the weak performance of a single member in a match to achieve victory. That is, teamwork proves to be the basis of success in work.
4. *Optimising the use of resources*: Each team member brings a unique set of capabilities, and the outcome is achieved by utilising each person's contributions.

Current state

All over India, people know lagori as a fun street game, but even then, the game's popularity is declining. We rarely find groups of children deciding to play at the spur of the moment.

Lagori is, however, now recognised as a team sport, and it is increasingly being played at international and national tournaments as organised events.

In India, official matches are organised by the Amateur Lagori Federation of India (ALFI), a national-level body, set up to promote the sport. It has about 300,000 players at the school level and over 500 match officials within the country. State lagori federations affiliated with ALFI are there in 24 states.

The International Lagori Federation, founded in 2010, has 17 countries as its members. The first championship was held in Bhutan in June 2013, in which 9 countries participated.

Variations of the game

Originally played on grassy or sandy open fields, the game has now evolved to indoor facilities. The randomly picked flat stones used to form a lagori have been replaced by nine specially made circular fibre discs.

Following are the few rules added by the International Lagori Federation:

1. Each team must consist of 12 players. However, only 6 players get on the field to play for every inning.
2. Each inning lasts for 3 minutes, and a 30-second break is given after each set.
3. The match has three sets, and the team that scores the maximum points in total is declared the winner.
4. No player is allowed to run with the ball. They have to throw it at the breakers or pass it to their teammates.
5. Once the lagori is broken, the nine discs have to be rearranged in the same order.

Glossary

lagori	Stack of seven flat discs—nine for international competitions
breakers	Toss-winning team, which will get the first chance to strike the lagori
defenders	Team that will field to tag the breakers
striker	Breaker who is striking the lagori at the given moment
breaking	To disrupt the stack of discs with a throw of the ball

3

Nondi

કુંડાળા

பாண்டி ஆட்டம்

ਪੀਚੋ ਬਕਰੀ

स्टापू

తొక్కుడుబిళ్ళ

Hopscotch

Introduction

Invented in the region around today's Tamil Nadu and widely played in rural parts of India and Sri Lanka, *nondi* is a hopping game with simple rules. Ancient Tamil literature has several references to a version of this game being played as *pandi attam* in temples across southern India. The game's concept is to avoid stepping on lines while leaping through a specific pattern drawn on the ground. Many variations of the game are popular around the world with different names. The English name hopscotch refers to hopping over the *scotch*—an incised line on the ground.

The game is also played in many other countries with large numbers of immigrant Indians. Hence, there are many varieties in the shapes of the grid designs.

Other names

Table 3.1

Region	*Name*	*Region*	*Name*
Tamil Nadu	*Nondi, Pandi attam*	Philippines, Vietnam	*Piko*
Karnataka	*Kunte bille*	Poland	*Klasy*
Kerala	*Vattu kali*	Spain	*Rayuela*
Gujarat	*Kundala, pagathiya, thikariya*	Norway	*Pradis*
Kashmir	*Saz Loung*	Bengal	*Ekka dukka*
Punjab	*Stapu, Peecho bakree*	Italy	*Campana, mondo*
Andhra Pradesh	*Tangidi billa*	Netherlands	*Hinkelen*
South Korea	*Ttangttamŏkki*	Bosnia, Croatia	*Skolica*
Afghanistan	*Cheendro*	Russia	*Kraccuku*
Turkey	*Sek sek*	Mexico	*Bebeleche*
Romania	*Sotron*	Brazil	*Amarelinha*
Malaysia	*Teng teng*	New York	*Potsy*
Cuba	*Pon*	Syria	*Hajla*
Germany, Austria, Switzerland	*Himmel und holle*	Glasgow, Edinburgh	*Peevers*

The play

For each player, the aim is to capture all the numbered circles drawn on the ground—at first, targeting them by throwing a marker, and then hopping through the series of circles to bring it back while balancing on one foot and without stepping on any lines. The goal for each player is to finish the series faster than others. However, there is no fixed number of turns or the duration of the game.

Number of players

The number can vary from two to six. Any number of players can join the game, but the larger the number of players, the longer it will take to get the next turn to play. At one time, only one player is on the go, and the rest watch. Therefore, if there are many players, then it could be boring to wait to get one's turn.

For speed nondi competitions, we draw several patterns and have several players play simultaneously in a separate series and note the time taken to finish the course for each player.

Equipment

1. A piece of chalk or chalk powder or masking tape is required to mark the nondi patterns on the floor.
2. A coin, a small slate stone, a pebble or a bottle cap is needed as a marker—usually not bigger than 3 in—for players to throw to mark the circle.

3. Nondi is also known as *thikariya* in Gujarat because broken earthen pot pieces called *thikra* are slid across the grid as a marker. Also, in New York, they call the game 'potsy'. The term probably refers to a potsherd that was used as a marker.

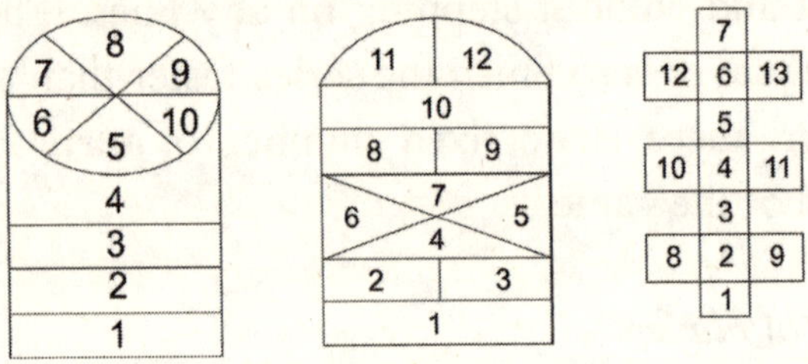

FIG. 3.1. Different patterns of the hopping series

Playground

School playgrounds, house backyards or street pavements—any ground without potholes or other serious damages can be used as a field. Slippery or very smooth surfaces should be avoided as they may cause the players to slip. For a single grid, an area of 5 ft x 18 ft should be adequate.

Drawing pattern

Nondi is played on a series of connected circles, rectangles and parallelograms drawn with chalk on pavements and numbered 1 to 8. There are several configurations, and the numbers change accordingly. We can use masking tape to outline the pattern on an indoor floor also. Each segment is about 2 ft in diameter/length, large enough to land comfortably with both feet and also that the marker thrown into a circle does not bounce out of it too easily. The drawing pattern measures about 15 ft x 4 ft as a whole court.

The most popular street pattern with circles (kundala) is illustrated next.

It is common to designate the ninth circle shown in the figure as a safe or stop area. This circle allows players to pause and take a moment to turn around and regain their balance before continuing the reverse move. This section is called 'home' or 'rest area'.

FIG. 3.2. Standard series pattern widely used in India

Playing method

Round I

1. Each player keeps a marker. The first player starts playing, and the other players will observe the play.
2. The active player stands outside the grid near Circle I and throws the marker inside the first circle. The marker should land inside the designated circle without bouncing or sliding out of the boundary.

If it lands on the wrong circle or on the boundary lines, then the player is out and passes the play to the next player.

3. While the marker lands inside Circle 1, the player hops through the court starting behind Circle 1 but jumps over Circle 1 (the one with the marker) for the first step and proceeds through the series. The player jumps one circle at a time without stepping on any line. If the player steps on a line or outside it, then they are out.
4. Players can choose to start with either foot but cannot land both feet on a single circle. When landing on two adjacent circles, they must land on one foot in each circle—the left foot in the left circle and the right foot in the right circle. In Circles 4-5 and 7-8, players can land with both feet.
5. When the player reaches the end of the series (Circles 7 and 8), they must turn around at once with a jump and start hopping back on one foot, in reverse order. When they reach Circle 2 (right before Circle 1, which has the marker), they must pause, lean down, standing on one foot still, and pick the marker up. Then, they must skip over Circle 1 and finish up the series.
6. If successful, the player's turn continues, and he or she now attempts to toss the marker to the next circle, Circle 2, and repeats the course till all the eight circles are completed.

As the distance to each circle increases, it becomes increasingly harder to throw the marker inside it. So the last few segments generally take more tries to capture, while the slower players get a chance to catch up.

This game is played at leisure, usually without time limits, for recreation. It is not considered a highly competitive sport, though there are winners and losers. The fun quotient is high, and so is the level of physical effort.

Round 2

1. Active players place the marker on the palm and keep the palm open and facing up.
2. Then they hop, starting from Circles 1 to 8, and pause in the home circle (ninth circle).
3. From the home circle, the players toss the marker ahead outside the series in the direction they were proceeding. Then they jump on the marker from the home circle with one foot and pause.
4. These steps are repeated with the coin on the inverted palm.

Round 3

After finishing round 2, the active players will stand outside the series near the home circle with the marker, facing away from the series. Now, they proceed to round 3.

1. The active player asks other players to choose *kaaya* or *pazhalama*, meaning the position of sitting or standing.
   a. If the other players (any one or collectively) shout 'kaaya', the player sits down near the home circle (Circle 9). Facing away from the series

and without looking at it, the player throws the marker over the head to aim at one of the circles. Note: The decision to select *kaaya* or *pazhalama* is not strategic to winning points. Hence, a suggestion by any player is usually accepted by the other players. However, if there is a conflict, a vote can be taken, or a coin can be tossed.

b. If the other players select *pazhalama*, then active players stand facing away from the series and throw the marker behind them, over the head and without looking, aiming at one of the circles.

c. Active players draw a cross in the circle in which the marker has landed. Then they pick up the marker and hop out of the series (ending near Circle 1). This success indicates that the player has captured that circle where the marker landed. In this circle, the player can land with both feet during the game from then onwards. Other players, however, while jumping through the circles, have to skip the circles which the current player owns.

2. At the end of each set of three rounds, the player can capture any one of the circles in the series. All the players will go through all three rounds again to capture the remaining circle. They can rest both feet in adjacent circles and in the circles that they have captured. Each player has to complete all three rounds again to capture another circle.

Hence, after every set of three rounds, the players make the game more challenging for others by taking away the freedom to land in the circles they have captured.

At the same time, it is easier for the players who own more segments as they can land with both feet.

Rules

1. The player who finishes the whole series first will be the winner of the first round.
2. The players who are out can restart play in the next turn from where they last left off (even the next day if there is no time left).
3. The winner of the third round is the player who captures the most circles and draws a cross in them to own them. The game may continue for a few sessions on different days to complete round 3.
4. For a short duration of play, you can set a stopwatch for each player and play only the first round. The player who completes the most circles in the set time is the winner.
5. A player loses turn at any stage, if
   a. While hopping through the course in either direction, the player steps on a line, hops on the wrong circle, skips a circle or goes out of the circle.
   b. He lands on a circle with a cross in it that has been captured by the other players (after the third round).
   c. The marker falls on or outside the grid lines of the grid or slips off the palm in the second round.
   d. The marker falls out of the series while tossing it from the home section in round 3.

Positions, tasks and techniques

TABLE 3.2

Roles	*Positions*	*Tasks*	*Strategy | Techniques*
The player on the move	Stand with a marker near Circle 1, facing the series ahead. Be ready to start the turn.	Throw the marker. Jump through the circles as per the rules.	Select a flat marker that is heavy and small, so it does not roll or skid much. Develop precision with the exact force needed to place the marker in the designated circle.
Other players	Stand near the series to closely observe the play.	Observe the playing teammate, and catch for fouls. Wait for one's turn patiently.	The player who can remember the level and the circle number where each player reached before getting ruled out is believed to be the smartest player and keenest observer.

Key skills required

The judgement of aiming at the right circle while throwing the marker is the primary skill. Then comes the ability to jump and the skill of balancing on one foot. Players must negotiate the circles and assess the needed force to jump for each leap so as not to step on the circle boundaries.

Any person who can keep the body balanced while hopping on one foot can enjoy the game. Men and women of all ages, and children above the age of five, can enjoy this game without any prior training or special skills. Not many tools or equipment is required to play it, and hence, it is popular during school vacations. It also can be played in the short duration of a school recess or as a street game for extended hours as the set-up time is insignificant. There is no set time limit for completing a game.

Caution

Nondi is generally not played in the hot sun during summer. In addition to players feeling the heat, the grounds become hot and may burn the feet as the game is generally played barefoot. The play area should be even without any potholes or pebbles to avoid injuries while hopping. Playing in very damp, sticky, muddy areas in the rainy season is not advisable either, as the players may slip.

Skills developed

1. The game improves agility and hand-eyes-feet coordination and enhances concentration.
2. It provides good exercise for the calf and leg muscles. It also helps children to manage body rhythm and body conditioning, which is the core skill, by hopping with precision and bending while standing on one foot.
3. According to a study published in the *European Journal of Sports Physiology*,[1] hopscotch improves the performance of long-distance runners as it

[1] https://synergians.wordpress.com/tag/exercise/

produces a range of limb movements and increases the flexibility of lower leg muscles.

Life lessons

1. Players learn to follow instructions and have the patience to wait for their turn while observing others play.
2. This game can be played alone too, and children learn self-discipline while following the rules.
3. This game has no opponents and no teams either. So the children learn to enjoy the play and play against themselves by improving timing, strength and precision. They also learn to compete and honour the efforts and achievements of others, and not to intrude in other's areas.

Current state

The fastest game was completed in 1 minute and 1.97 seconds by an American, Ashrita Furman, in November 2010.[2] The longest game, measuring 6,131 m, was created by the Chinese brand Teenmix of Belle International in Guangzhou in Guangdong, China, in 2016. The course consisted of 1,518 standard games, and over 300 participants took part in the two-day event. Five of them finished the entire game, with the fastest player completing in 8 hours and 55 minutes.[3]

[2] https://www.guinnessworldrecords.com/world-records/fastest-game-of-hopscotch

[3] https://www.guinnessworldrecords.com/world-records/longest-hopscotch-game/

Variations of the game

Several configurations are possible, constrained only by creativity. As this game can be played by a single player as well, one can create patterns and rules accordingly.

1. *Change the drawing pattern*: You can make rectangular or triangular sections or draw them in a zigzag pattern, with the numbers going in a spiral direction. In France, they call it *escargot*—the French word for snail. Start drawing from the middle and go outwards, making the shapes bigger as you go outward. The player hops on one foot on each circle all the way through the spiral and back.

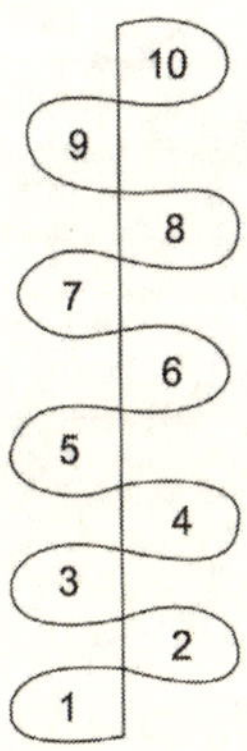

FIG. 3.3. Zigzag series

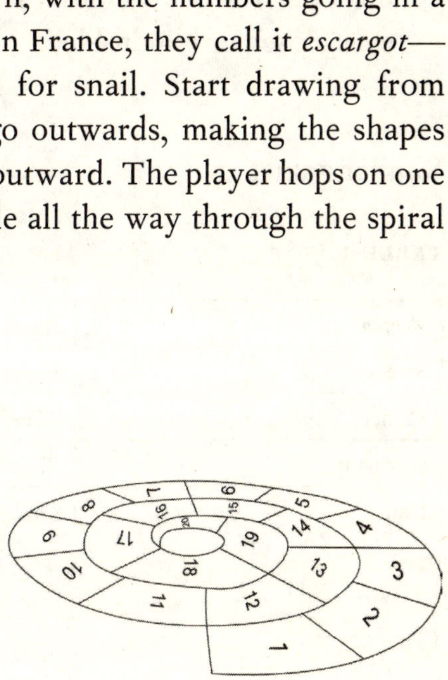

FIG. 3.4. Escargot

2. *Set a time limit*: Make it a rapid nondi. Set the stopwatch for 30 to 50 seconds. Each player must complete the course within the time frame to proceed. You could turn it into a race, covering two or three patterns at the same time.

3. *Kick the marker*: The marker is typically picked up in the game, but historically, it was kicked sequentially back through the grid on the reverse move and then kicked out. You may try kicking the marker from circle to circle while hopping back in the series.
4. *The ultimate pandi*: This variation is the toughest stage of nondi and is only played by more experienced players. The players have to hop through a series of circles/rectangles with their eyes closed or blindfolded.

Similar games

TABLE 3.3

Region	*Name*
Sweden	*Hoppa hage*
France	*Marelles*
Germany	*Templehufen*
Iran	*Laylay, Khane bazi*

Glossary

marker	Coin, small slate stone, pebble or bottle cap that players throw to mark a circle
kaaya	Sitting posture
pazhalama	Standing posture

4

Nalugu Rallu Atta

મરઘી નું ઈંડુ

நாலுமூலைக் கல

నాలుగు రాళ్ల ఆట

Steal the egg
Game of four stones

Introduction

Nalugu rallu atta is a recreational street game—a popular form of the run-and-catch-sport played in a relatively small playfield. It was widely played until the late 1980s in rural and urban areas of India. Originating from Andhra Pradesh, this game is based on swiftly stealing four stones from the centre of the court, which are guarded by the chaser, while escaping the tag and reaching safe zones with the teammates.

Other names

TABLE 4.1

Region	*Name*	*Region*	*Name*
Tamil Nadu	*Naalu moolai kal*	Gujarat	*Marghi nu eendu*
Andhra Pradesh	*Nalugu rallu aata*	United States of America, United Kingdom	Steal the egg/ Four stones

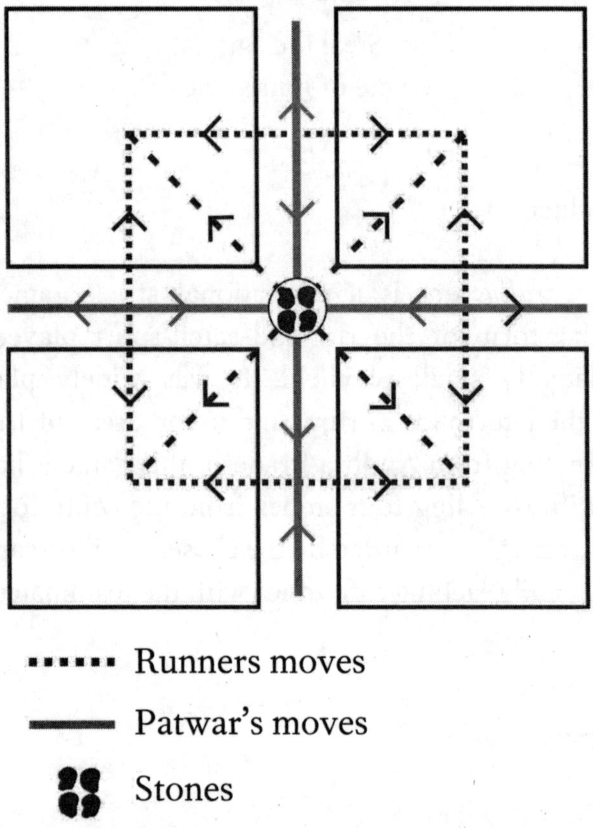

FIG. 4.1. Diagram of the play area and players' moves

The play

At the beginning, four runners take their positions in one square each, and four stones are placed in a circle drawn in the middle. The runners must steal the stones and bring them to their respective squares without being captured by the patwar (chaser). Then, they must collect all the stones in any one of the squares. The patwar's aim is to capture the runners while they are on the move.

Number of players

There are five players. Of them, one will be selected to be the patwar. So there are four runners and one patwar.

The playground

Four independent square boxes of sides measuring 5 ft are drawn, leaving tracks of about 2 ft between them, on an open flat playground measuring around 12 ft x 12 ft At the intersection of the paths between the squares, a circle is drawn with a 6 in diameter. Four medium-sized stones are placed in that circle.

Equipment needed

A chalk or white powder is required to mark the boundaries, and four small stones of any shape and size are needed. You may use any substitute available for the stones, such as small rubber balls or tiny wood logs.

Playing method

1. The players' names are written on pieces of paper, and the player whose name is picked becomes the patwar. This way, the patwar is randomly chosen at the start of the game. Players can choose any other method as well in an informal game.
2. The other four players stand in the four boxes (one in each), which they occupy as their native houses.
3. The play begins when the patwar starts cutting the four tracks one by one—touching the end lines and returning to the centre quickly. In doing so, the patwar has to leave the centre and go till the end of the court four times, moving in the tracks only in the space between the square houses. Meanwhile, the runners try to take one or more or even all four stones placed at the centre without being caught by the patwar.
4. After cutting the tracks, the patwar keeps moving along the cross-section to capture the runners who try to steal the stones. The patwar is not supposed to enter the boxes.
5. One of the players can also pick up all four stones and then move into other boxes, distributing the stones to the remaining three runners. Only one player need not necessarily take the initiative to collect all the stones. Any runner can pick up as many stones as they can for distribution.
6. When each runner has at least one stone each, there is no need for distribution.

7. When all the runners get their stone, running and chasing stops. Runners ask the patwar to choose either *gumpu* (group) or *chhuttu* (separate).
    a. If the patwar says gumpu and selects a particular box, then all other players gather in that box with the stones in their hands. The patwar can tag any runner anytime when they move close enough.
    b. If the choice is chhuttu, each runner has to make three rounds starting from the present box and finally reach his or her native box while escaping the patwar's touch. The patwar can tag any runner while they are moving across the boxes to settle in their respective boxes.
8. In both the gumpu and chhuttu options, if the patwar catches any of the four runners, he or she will be the new patwar of the next game.
9. The game continues for the next two innings with all five players, and the winner is declared after all the three innings are played.

Scoring

One set of the game consists of three innings with the same five players. The winner is the runner who is not caught during all three innings of the game and escapes being the patwar every time.

Rules

1. One box can be occupied by only one player as a house (native square).
2. The patwar can move only along the cross sections between the squares, horizontally or vertically, but cannot enter any squares or go out of the boundary.
3. The other players can move in all directions, through the squares and in cross sections within the boundary.
4. When the patwar's choice is gumpu for the second round, all the players will gather in one box if and only if they have acquired their stone—one stone each.
5. The game continues until all the four players gather in one square with all the four stones. In chhuttu, all players must reach their native squares after running three rounds, passing through all four squares and escaping the tag by the patwar.
6. If a player is tagged out as per the rules, then he or she becomes the new patwar, and the former patwar will join the other runners. The game then starts again with the same rules.
7. If the patwar catches one of the runners while they are moving through four boxes, the runner is declared out and becomes the next patwar in the new game.
8. If the runners successfully grab all four stones and pass both rounds, they get the chance to be runners again. The same patwar will be the chaser in the next game.

Positions, tasks and techniques

TABLE 4.2

Roles	*Positions*	*Tasks*	*Strategy / Techniques*
Patwar	Stand at the intersection of the tracks, and guard the stones placed at the centre.	At the start, cut the tracks, reach the border on the four sides and return to the centre immediately to mind the stones. Catch the runners who attempt to steal the stones. Catch as many runners as possible.	Be vigilant of the runners' attempts to steal the stones from all four sides. It is easier to catch them when they are close to the centre. Keep changing directions rapidly and unpredictably.
Runners	Take positions, one player in each house.	Watch the patwar's moves and position and attempt to steal the stones. Pick as many as possible, but the stones would have to be distributed too. Save oneself from the tag while moving from house to house.	It is easier to grab all the stones at once and distribute them than each player taking the risk of being tagged out while going near the patwar to take them individually. Stealing the stones from the centre by misdirecting the patwar's attention requires feinting movements and swift snatching techniques.

Key skills required

Swift reflex actions are critical in the game. Stealing the stones from the centre and distributing them among the other team members needs rapid decision making and fast running.

Children between eight to fifteen years of age enjoy the game, but men and women of any age can participate in the game. It can be played by five individuals of any age who possess adequate running speeds and agility in catching the players. No training-based gameplay is involved for any player in this game, thus making it more enjoyable for older adults.

It is a typical fun vacation game that involves the struggle of stealing the stones from the chaser's security.

Cautions

The playing area should be flat and smooth to avoid stumbling while playing, as this game is normally played barefoot. An area with slippery surfaces, wet mud or big potholes or rocks may hurt the players.

Skills developed

The game develops cognitive skills, including rapid reflex actions, quick responses, swift decisions and focused attention. Moreover, it makes children agile, fast runners and keen observers.

Life lessons

The pivotal element of the game is stealing the stones and then distributing them to all the players. Each team member knows that everyone has to have the stone. Until then, they cannot win. The game teaches working as a team and making timely decisions in favour of the whole team while, at the same time, saving oneself from getting tagged out.

Current state

Informal groups of children in the village areas of Gujarat, Andhra Pradesh and Karnataka enjoy playing this exciting game on the streets.

Variations of the game

You may omit the last phase of selecting gumpu or chhuttu and keep only gumpu as a standard final stage of the game. For quick arrangements, you can use shoes or slippers instead of stones.

Similar games

Nalugu stambalata (Andhra Pradesh)

In this game, instead of the four squares, the runners occupy four pillars of the house or corridor—one pillar for each player as their respective homes. The runners must shift from one pillar to the other without being caught, and the chaser has to capture the runners while they shift from pillar to pillar.

Glossary

houses	Four square boxes that are assigned one to each runner
patwar	Player who is selected to be a chaser
gumpu	All the runners gather in one box (as a group)
chhuttu	All the four runners distributed in their respective houses (separated)

5

Yubi Lakpi (Manipuri Rugby)

Introduction

Yubi lakpi is an outdoor game that originated in Manipur, and even today, it is played primarily in Manipur. It is an intense sport, played especially during the Sangai festival that showcases the region's traditional music, dances and games. This game predates and resembles the games played with an oval ball, such as American football or British rugby. However, unlike these Western games, Yubi lakpi involves martial arts like *Mukna*—the *Meitie* wrestling.

The name is also of Manipuri origin: *yubi* means coconut, and *lakpi* means to grab. Literally, yubi lakpi means 'coconut snatching'.

Other names

The game is also known as Manipuri rugby.

The play

This game engages the players in a struggle to snatch an unpeeled, oil-soaked coconut, which they have to carry through the goal at the other end of the field. Snatching and holding the coconut is challenging as players are smeared with a mixture of mustard oil and water before the game starts. This mixture of oil and water makes them slippery for the opponents to catch and hold.

It is a game of individuals because each player attempts to win the coconut and get the reward. There are no opposing teams and no fixed time duration for the competition. The individual player plays against all the remaining players at all times.

Traditionally, after battling the other players, the snatched coconut is presented to the chief of the tribe. The chief would observe the play and notice the most skilful and strongest player. Each player, therefore, put in all their efforts to get noticed for possessing battlefield qualities. Nowadays, the chief is often a teacher, a chief guest or an official.

The playground

The sport is played on a rectangular field, about 45 m x 18 m in dimensions. Going lengthwise, one end of the field has a 4.5 m x 3 m box area after the finish line, known as the goal region. The goal region is mostly indicated by a pole or two pieces of white cloth rolled up to look like a flag. There is only one goalpost.

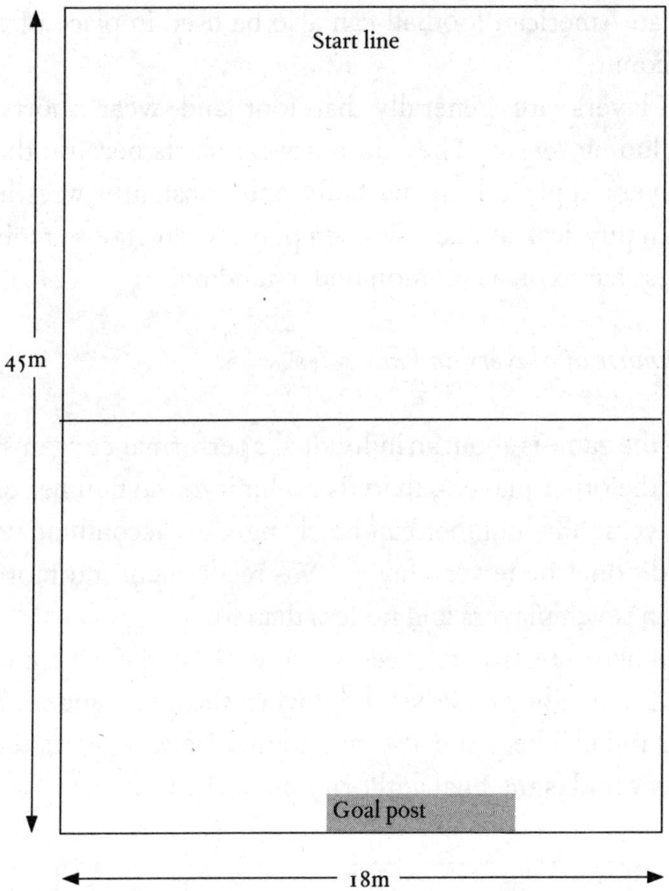

FIG. 5.1. Playground for yubi lakpi

The playground may vary based on the discretion of the game organisers. It is mostly played on rough, dried mud. Alternatively, it can be played on a grass field.

Material required

Lime powder or chalk sticks to mark boundaries, mustard oil and coconut are required. A rugby ball or an American football can also be used in place of a coconut.

Players are generally barefoot and wear shorts, including *langot*. They do not wear shirts because the players apply oil on the body and constantly wrestle with physical contact. Women players can choose their dress based on a common understanding.

Number of players and key roles

As the game is about an individual's performance against all the other players, there is no limit to the number of players. The number can be changed to accommodate additional or fewer players. We recommend no more than seven players and no less than four.

There are two referees—one each at the start and end line. They observe and govern the game and look for fouls. The game also has an umpire who starts the game and is the final authority on decisions.

FIG. 5.2. The game in action

Playing method

1. The players assemble behind the start line outside the boundary of the playground.
2. The game starts with the referee placing the coconut inside the playground, near the start line. Immediately after that, the referee signals the start of the game with a whistle. The players rush inside the playground, and each one attempts to grab the coconut.
3. The player who grabs the coconut holds it to the chest and runs towards the goal, manoeuvring to avoid getting caught by the opponents.
4. As soon as the player with the coconut starts running, the others rush to push him or her to the ground. Once down, the player tries to get up, but the others storm over to push the player down, each trying to snatch the coconut. But the player with the coconut makes every effort to hold on to it. It requires a great deal of energy, fitness and stamina to endure extensive strain.
5. When another player snatches the coconut, that player now rushes towards the finish line. The process of rushing and catching begins all over again with the new player as the target. Then the coconut is snatched by yet another player, and the game continues.
6. With each new player getting the coconut, the group reaches closer to the goalpost. While the game may appear simple, it is difficult to get a noticeable breakthrough and reach the goalpost, considering each player is slippery and hard to hold. After several tussles, one of the players gets to the goalpost.

7. At this final stage, an intense struggle occurs when one of the players slips away with the coconut after defending against all the players. Such escapes require agility and strength.
8. Once a goal is achieved, the game is over.
9. The winner offers the coconut to the chief or the judges sitting just beyond the goal line.
10. The next round of the game can start, and will keep going for pre-defined time, say 30 minutes or till the players agree to play.

Scoring

No scoring points or team structure is applied in this game. The player who reaches the goal box first with the coconut is the sole winner. The game starts fresh again for the next innings.

Rules

1. Players must hold the coconut against their chest or carry it under their arm. It must touch the body at all times.
2. Players cannot kick, punch or beat the opponents or tackle players who do not have the coconut.
3. Players cannot kick the coconut. The coconut must be carried with the players all the way to the goal.
4. Players are allowed to tackle only the player carrying the coconut. They cannot hinder or obstruct other runners.

5. The player who reaches the goal box while in possession of the coconut is the winner.

Optionally, the coconut is later offered to the chief or the judge. The winner is also often awarded the coconut as the prize.

Position, tasks and techniques

TABLE 5.1

Roles	*Positions*	*Tasks*	*Strategy / Techniques*
The player in possession of the coconut	Be on the run with the coconut.	Rush towards the goal line, defending against all the other players.	Keep changing the direction of running, and move unpredictably. Swiftly change the style of body moves, and confuse the opponents about the next move.
Players pursuing the coconut	Be on the run. Chase the player with the coconut.	Try to retrieve the coconut by snatching, running fast and pushing.	Attack the player with the coconut from an angle that provides maximum resistance to the active player and offers the least resistance from the other chasers.

FIG. 5.3. Players reach near the goalpost. The chief is seated in the chair.

Key skills required

The game requires a great deal of vigorous body play, stamina and endurance and demands wrestling ability, speed and excellent reflexes. An alert mind and calmness under pressure are needed as well. It is tough to move forward with the coconut, even for a few steps, if the player is not strong and skilled compared to the opponents.

Players of any age and gender with stamina and combat skills can participate in this game. The dress code can be modified to suit the players.

Caution

To prevent stumbling while running fast, the playground surface should be even without bumps or potholes.

To prevent injuries, the players should not hinder the movements of the other players. The players should not push other teammates out of the boundary.

The game is normally played by individuals with strength and stamina and can be risky for relatively less-skilled players.

Skills developed

Yubi lakpi enhances reflex actions like dodging and feinting. Players become more alert and aware of surrounding traps that can hold them back. This game develops physiological strength by exercising leg and hand muscles. Also, fast running and quick decision making are the key skills gained.

Life lessons

Yubi lakpi is a game of individuals because each player tries to win the coconut and get the reward. In the original ancient games, the king would watch the players to see who was the most skilful and possessed qualities for the battlefield. Therefore, each player would try to impress and strive to be fit for any struggle or fights in life.

Current state

The movie director Omung Kumar and the producer Sandeep Ssingh of *Mary Kom* and *Sarbjit* fame are collaborating to make a sports drama, *Yubi Lakpi*, indicating that the game is gaining traction.

An official game is held on the occasion of the five-day *Yaoshang* festival in the presence of the Manipuri royal family. Yaoshang, a mini Olympiad, is a platform for channelising young talents and improving harmonious socialisation among the locals.

Origin

Largely unexplored and undisturbed, north-east India has a diverse culture of traditional sports and festivals. Yubi lakpi is traditionally associated with native forms of Hinduism. It is said to have started as a ceremonial re-enactment of the celestial grabbing of the pot of nectar after the *Samudra Manthan*.

Emma Levine, an English writer on little-known Asian sports, speculates:

> Perhaps this was the root of modern rugby? Most Manipuris are quite adamant that the modern world 'stole' the idea from them and made it into rugby.... This game, which has been around for centuries, is so similar to rugby, which evolved a great deal later, that it must be more than a coincidence.[1]

Variations of the game

1. In ancient times, the group played as two teams, and it was not necessary to have an equal number of players in both teams. The players of the team that possesses the coconut were allowed to prevent the opponents who are hindering the move towards the goal.
2. Players need not oil their bodies or play bare-chested; they can wear regular sports attire. Then this game can be played during school breaks.

[1] htpps://ipfs.io/ipfs/QmXoypizjW3WknFiJnKLwHCnL72vedxjQkD-DP1mXWo6uco/wiki/Rugby_union_in_India.html

Similar games

TABLE 5.2

Region	*Name*
Australia	Man grook
China	*Cuju*
The United Kingdom	Rugby
Argentina, Colombia, Costa Rica, Ecuador, Guatemala, Honduras, Nicaragua, Panama, Uruguay and Spain	*Rayuela*
Italy	*Calcio fiorentino*
Ghana	*Tumatu*

Glossary

yubi	Coconut
lakpi	To grab or snatch
jatra	King of the land or head of the institution

6

Gilli Danda

घातिका

ગિલ્લી ડંડો

கிட்டிப்புள்

डण्डी बियो

ਡਾਙਗੁੱਲ਼ੀ ਡੰਡਾ

ಚಿನ್ನಿ ಕೋಲು

ଗୁଲି ବାଡ଼ି

കുട്ടിയും കോലും

विट्टी दांडू

ডাংগুটি

Tip-cat

Introduction

The game of striking a small tapered wooden stick called *gilli* with a long stick has been popular in India for about 5,000 years. It is believed to have been spread by the Maurya empire about 2,500 years ago to today's Sindh, Afghanistan, Nepal, Bangladesh, Cambodia, Italy, some parts of Turkey and Africa. This game is also said to be the precursor of American baseball and British cricket.

Other names

TABLE 6.1

Region	*Name*	*Region*	*Name*
Ancient India	*Ghaṭikā*	Bengal	*Danguli khela*
Kerala	*Kuttiyum kolum*	Karnataka	*Chinni kolu*
Bihar	*Guli tan*	Maharashtra	*Viti dandu*
Gujarat	Gulli dando	Meghalaya	*Beh dieing khun*
Kashmir	*Lathkeeji-loth*	Multan	*Geeti danna*
Tamil Nadu	*Kitti pullu*	Punjab	*Gulli danda*
Telangana	*Chirra gonay*	Assam	*Tan guti*
Andhra Pradesh	*Billam godu, Gooti billa*	Odisha	*Guli badi, Guti dabula*
USA	Tip-cat	Sindh	*Iti daka*
Nepal	*Dandi biyo*	Konkan	*Koyondo-bal*
Cambodia	*Kon ko*	Indonesia	*Pathel lele*
Turkey	*Çelik comak*	Vietnam	*Đánh trỏng, Đánh khăng*
Myanmar	*Ciang sat*	Philippines	*Awe etew*
Italy	*Lippa*	Cuba	*Quimbumbia*
Afghanistan	*Lappa duggi*	Iran	*Alak doulak*

The play

The goal is to strike the gilli to drive it the farthest distance possible without it getting caught by the opponents. The striker scores by measuring the distance covered by the gilli from the striking point. After the gilli has been struck, the opponents attempt to catch it in mid-air before it hits the ground.

Equipment

The game is played with two wooden sticks:

1. *Gilli*: This stick is 4 in to 6 in long with a diameter of 1 in to 1.5 in, tapered on both sides. At both ends of the stick, the diameter is about one-third of the middle part.
2. *Danda*: This stick is 1.5 ft to 2 ft long and 1 in diameter. It is used for striking the gilli.

The gilli is tapered at both ends to allow for striking it, and the greatest challenge lies in how well and how far one can strike the spinning gilli in the air.

The playground

This game is played in the streets or any open ground, measuring about 60 m in length and 40 m in breadth. A formal sports ground is not necessary as one can draw informal boundary lines, and the dimensions can be adjusted to fit the space available.

For official matches, the playground dimensions vary from 40 m to 100 m in length with boundaries.

Number of players and key roles

The two teams have an equal number of players. Each team has between one to six players.

As evident, one person on each side can also play this game, but then the game would not have the variations and dynamism. There would also be fewer opportunities for the gilli to be caught. Similarly, for more than six players, players will have to wait longer for their turn, and it may be too easy for the opposing team to catch the gilli.

For an informal game, one captain for each team is selected. For official matches, there are two linemen and one umpire, along with a referee, a scorekeeper and a timekeeper.

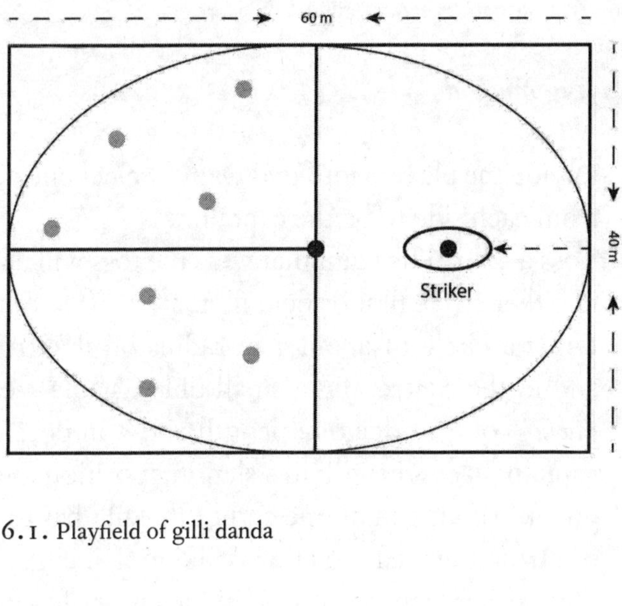

FIG. 6.1. Playfield of gilli danda

FIG. 6.2. Strike 2 when the gilli is in the air

Playing method

1. Divide the players into two teams. Select one player from each side to be the captain.
2. Toss a coin. The team that wins the toss will choose to either strike first or field first.
3. Draw a circle of about 2 m radius on the ground, and in the centre, dig a small oblong hole—called *guchi*—of 3 in diagonal length and 2 in deep. The captain places the gilli in a slanting position into the guchi. About 1 in of one end of the gilli has to stick out from the guchi to allow striking that edge.
4. The striker takes a position in the circle close to the guchi. The fielding team spreads out in the field to catch the gilli.
5. The striker lifts the gilli from the guchi by hitting its edge using the danda. A good hit tosses the gilli in the air. While it is in the air momentarily, the striker

hits the gilli with the danda again. He or she tries to make it go the farthest possible distance in the direction with the least chances of the gilli getting caught by the fielders.

6. If the striker tosses the gilli and any of the fielders catches before it touches the ground, the striker is declared out.
7. If the striker hits the gilli and no fielder catches it, the game proceeds. The striker hits the gilli again, striking it from the ground to lift it up and quickly hitting it again to send it as far as possible and away from the fielders.
8. Each striker can strike the gilli three times to move it forward: once to lift it from the guchi, then while it is in the air and finally from the place the gilli reached after the second hit.
9. The distance from the circle to the point where the gilli lands is measured using the danda. If the player cannot hit the gilli in three continuous chances, the turn is over. Now, the next player of the same team gets a turn.
10. The same set of steps are repeated until all the players of the striker team are out. Then the roles are exchanged, and the fielding team will be on strike.
11. The steps remain the same for the new strikers. The second innings begins with chasing the opponents' score.
12. The final score of the team will be a total of the points gained by all the players. The team with the higher score will win the match.
13. This game can be played individually too, where each player plays against the rest, and the highest point earner wins. This format is often preferred when the total number of players is small, say, less than six.

14. Team captains usually serve as referees as well. The captain on the opposite team watches for violations and fouls.

Scoring

1. The points a striker scores are measured by the distance the gilli covers from the guchi circle. The player gets one point for each length of the danda between the circle and the gilli. The striker gains as many points as the length measured in the unit of the danda.
2. Players can also set a unit for scoring, such as 3 danda = 1 point.
3. Scoring also depends on how many times the gilli was hit in the air in one strike. The gilli can be struck twice mid-air by expert players. If it travels a certain distance with two mid-air strikes, the total points are doubled.

Rules

1. If the gilli falls inside the circle after being struck, then the striker is out. If not, the striker gets another chance to hit the gilli.
2. The striking player is out in the following situations:
    a. If the gilli happens to fall and hit the danda again after striking;
    b. If the gilli is caught by the fielding team after the strike;
    c. When the striker hits the gilli and it falls behind the guchi.

3. After every strike, the captain measures the distance that the gilli reached. Once the distance is measured and noted, then the next player can take their turn.

Positions, tasks and techniques

TABLE 6.2

Roles	*Positions*	*Tasks*	*Strategy | Techniques*
Striker	Take a position with the danda in the circle, near the guchi.	Hit the gilli with the danda, flipping the gilli up from the guchi, and strike it again mid-air.	Strike the gilli at a precise angle. Strike the gilli just below its centre of gravity to get a 45 degrees projection, or better, strike at the centre when the gilli is making an angle of about 45 degrees from vertical.
Fielders	Take positions at locations that offer the maximum chances of catching the gilli.	Catch the gilli in the air before it lands on the ground.	Observe the striker to gauge the direction the gilli will fly.
Referee	Stand away from the circle to observe the play.	Watch the striker and fielders for any foul play. Measure the distance from the guchi to where the gilli falls.	Stand in the line of sight of the gilli after each strike.

Key skills required

Players need to assess the movement of fast-moving objects and be able to hit precisely when a unique opportunity is presented during the flight of the gilli. Strength is less important than precision as the gilli hit at the ends will travel only a short distance even if hit hard.

This game is generally played by children and adults of the ages between eight to twenty. However, individuals of all ages and genders can participate equally easily. This game does not involve running, which makes it easy to play by older persons as well.

Caution

The play can be risky because the gilli may go astray and hit an inattentive player or a passer-by. In addition, the gilli often gets lost in bushes, and the players need to watch for snakes and other animals while retrieving it.

Skills developed

The game helps build concentration and develops hand-eye coordination and hand-feet coordination for long-distance hitting. It helps to improve the precision of hitting.

In addition, players develop skills for estimating the position and orientation of a fast-moving object. It improves the assessment of the dynamics of movements.

Players also learn the basic laws of motion, the trajectory of a projectile under the force of gravity and the transfer of momentum from the danda to the gilli.

Life lessons

Players develop skills for team coordination, leadership and conflict resolution.

Current state

This sport of the rural and small towns is still fairly popular in northern India. In 2016, the countries playing gilli danda came under the aegis of the Gilli Danda International Federation, headquartered in Noida in Uttar Pradesh. Nepal, Afghanistan, Brazil, Bhutan, Iran, Basque, Bangladesh, Pakistan, Taiwan, South Africa and Italy are members, in addition to India.

Since 2017, Gilli Danda has been included in the Ambedkar National games, and since 2018, it has been included in Gujarat *Khel Mahakumbh*, which includes participants from all over India.

Variations of the game

The Gilli Danda International Federation has approved rules with variations in scoring techniques, playground dimensions and playing methods, which are implemented for official matches.[1]

1 https://gillidandasport.com/

The major difference is that when the gilli becomes airborne after it is struck and lands on the ground, the fielder closest to the gilli has one chance to hit the danda (which is to be placed on the guchi) with a throw of the gilli (similar to a run out in cricket). The striker is out if the fielder is successful; if not, the striker scores one point and gets another opportunity to strike.

Similar games

TABLE 6.3

Region	*Name*	*Region*	*Name*
England	Giddy-gaddy	Philippines	*Pati-kubra*
South Korea	*Jachigi*	Mexico	*Changarais, Kimbomba*
Azerbaijan	*Chilingaghaj*	Slovenia	*Pandolfo*
Galicia, Spain	*Billarda*	China	*Da-ga-ga*
Catalonia and Valencia	*Bòlit*		

Glossary

gilli	Small wooden stick, about 4 in to 6 in long, crafted from a twig
danda	Long wooden stick to strike, 1.5 ft to 2 ft long and about 1 in diameter
guchi	Oblong hole dug in the ground, about a handspan long and 1 in wide

7

Nadee Parvat

नदी - पर्वत

નદી કે પર્વત

ऊँच-नीच का पापड़ा

ನೆಲ-ಬಂಡೆ

दगड का माती

डेंगा पानी

কুমির দাঙ্গা

Introduction

Popularly called *denga-paani*[1] and known as *nadee parvat* in many regions, this traditional run-and-chase game is from the state of Bihar. The terms used in the game are nadee or a ground area or lower surface like a river; parvat or an area higher than the ground level, like a mountain; and *magar*, the player who has to catch the other players, like a crocodile living in the river. The concept is that the magar tries to catch the other players when they enter the area designated for the magar. The

1 Denga means a boat. Nadee means river, magar means crocodile and parvat is a hill or mountain.

challenge for the other players is to venture out into the area which they do not occupy.

This game doesn't require a large playground, so it gained popularity in village streets. However, it can be played in urban areas as well.

Other names

TABLE 7.1

Region	*Name*	*Region*	*Name*
Andhra Pradesh	*Naela banda*	Bihar	*Denga-pani, Nehriya ki daab dubiya*
Gujarat	*Nadee ke parvat*	Maharashtra	*Dagad ka maati*
West Bengal	*Kumir danga*	Uttar Pradesh	*Unch neech ka papda*

The play

Equipment needed

No equipment is required for this game, except the demarcated playing area.

The playground

This simple outdoor game can be played in parks, on empty streets, just outside houses using the steps of the veranda or on any open ground with raised platforms—the lower level to be used as the nadee and the elevated level as the parvat. In case the ground with raised areas is not available, we may draw or mark several square boxes to designate them as the parvat, or raised platforms can be created simply by using bricks or flat stone sheets.

On a flat surface, an area of total size 30 ft x 20 ft with around four to six square boxes measuring 2 ft x 2 ft can be used as the parvat. The boxes are drawn scattered randomly throughout the play area.

Number of players

Any number of players can join the game depending on the space available. We recommend between four to eight players. The players who occupy the parvat are the runners.

FIG. 7.1. The magar catching the runners

Playing method

1. Select any player to be the magar and ask him or her to choose one of the two areas: nadee or parvat. The lower area is designated as the nadee. Usually, the magar

opts for nadee to run freely, and the runners occupy the higher areas of the ground. The game begins when one or more runners venture into the nadee and tease the magar with this song: *Hum tumhare pani me, pakdo* (I am in your area, catch me if you can).

2. When the runners enter the nadee, the magar chases them, and the runners get back on the parvat to save themselves. Any runner can take any parvat during the game as a safe area.
3. If the magar touches any part of a runner's body while he or she is in the nadee, then the magar gets two points, and the runner loses one point. The caught runner will now play the magar, and the next round of the game will continue.
4. If a runner is able to touch the magar's back without getting touched by the magar's hand, then the runner gains one point.
5. The players constantly move from the parvat to the nadee. The game is always fast-moving as all the players are on the move, coordinating and competing with others.

Scoring

If the magar catches a runner, the magar gets two points, and the caught runner loses one point (minus one). If a runner touches the magar's back, then the runner gains one point. In the end, the person with the highest score is the winner. Often, players choose to play without keeping score, and the game is still interesting as players rotate in their roles.

Rules

1. Once the magar chooses the nadee area, he or she should not step onto the parvat area by any means or let other players step on the nadee.
2. The players will have to move constantly in both areas. They cannot stand in the same position for more than 10 seconds; else, the play will be stagnant.
3. When the runners rush and try to touch the magar on the back, they should not push him or her. Otherwise, the magar may stumble and fall.

Positions, tasks and techniques

TABLE 7.2

Roles	*Positions*	*Tasks*	*Strategy | Techniques*
Magar (the chaser)	Take a position in nadee.	Catch the runners who intrude in the nadee area.	Be vigilant to catch the runners. Pretend to move in planned directions that appear to be random to divert their attention.
The runners	Take positions in areas designated as the parvat.	Venture into the magar's area, leaving the parvat. As a team, enter the nadee swiftly and escape, coordinating with other runners.	Enter into the magar's area from unpredictable directions to confuse the magar who is trying to catch the runners.

Key skills required

Any individual with adequate running speed and an alert mind can participate in the play. A player's success depends on agility and the ability to react quickly to a changed situation, such as a quick movement by other players or the magar.

Children of ages five to fifteen years primarily play this game. All genders and people of all ages enjoy this game, as physical strength is not critical. Corporate events and family gatherings are also ideal opportunities for adults to play this game.

Caution

The players need to be careful not to stumble on the ground while running and jumping through the two levels. In addition, since the space is limited, the players are likely to collide as well.

Skills developed

The players learn to decide quickly and to rapidly calculate the timing according to the game's pace. The game helps to analyse and choose the better option from two situations at the moment.

Life lessons

While playing this game, children learn to be alert and confident. To save their teammates from getting tagged out, they find new techniques to divert the rival's attention while he or she is chasing any one of the players.

Current state

The game is still considered a fun activity in schools during recess in some regions but has lost its charm as a traditional street game.

Variations of the game

Players recite the following phrases in their respective languages when they ask the magar for the choice.

In Marathi, they say, '*Kora kagad nili shai, amhi konhala bhiti nahi. Sanga tumcha nav kay, dagad ka maati?*'

In Gujarati, '*Maango, shu maangyu ... nadee ke parvat?*' '*Ame tamara pani ma, pakdo pakdo.*'

In Telugu, it is recited as '*Nee nelanta pappu suddha*'.

In Hindi, the question is translated as '*Unch neech ka papda—oonch mangi ki neech?*' Or, '*Hum tumhare pani me, pakado.*'

Glossary

nadee	Lower areas of the playfield
parvat	Raised platforms or higher areas of the playfield
runners	Players who are assigned to the parvat
magar	Chaser

8

Cheel Jhapatta

काक-काकातुआ

रुमाल छू

रुमाल झपट्टा

Dog and the bone
Steal the bacon

Introduction

Cheel jhapatta is a basic chasing game involving focused, swift actions where players snatch a rumal (handkerchief). The players have to grab the rumal, which is placed in the middle of the playing area, before their opponents can. Moreover, players have to simultaneously block the opponents from taking the rumal by forming a hand-fence and must chase the opponents if they have already picked it up. The movement is like a vulture snatching a piece of meat and flying away quickly.

Instead of a handkerchief, a small piece of cloth or a stone can also be used. This game has simple rules and basic difficulty levels for scoring. Therefore, only a limited strategic construct is required.

Other names

TABLE 8.1

Region	*Name*	*Region*	*Name*
Rajasthan	*Rumaal chori/ jhapatta*	Western countries	Dog and the bone
Punjab, Haryana, Uttar Pradesh	*Rumaal chhu*	United Kingdom, Europe	Steal the bacon
India (in Sanskrit)	*Kaak-kakatua*	Gujarat	*Cheel jhappat*

The play

The sequence of play involves the two players rushing quickly to the centre and hovering over the rumal, aiming to grab it the moment the opponent is distracted. The goal is to baffle the opponent by feinting and dodging to pick up the rumal. The player who has grabbed the rumal speeds away before the opponent can grab the player.

Number of players

There are two teams, six to twelve players each, and one referee.

Both the teams must have an equal number of players. The team captains or the referee check that the stronger and the weaker players are distributed fairly in both teams.

Material required

A handkerchief (rumal) or small rubber ball, beanbag or any other unbreakable object can be used. Even an empty bottle or a shoe can also be designated as the object to be snatched.

FIG. 8.1. Two opponents come forward to grab the rumal

Playground

The dimension of the ground is around 32 m in length and 12 m in breadth. The rumal is kept in the middle of the ground in a circle of 2 ft diameter. However, you may decrease or increase the playing area depending on the fitness of the players, the total number of players and the available space.

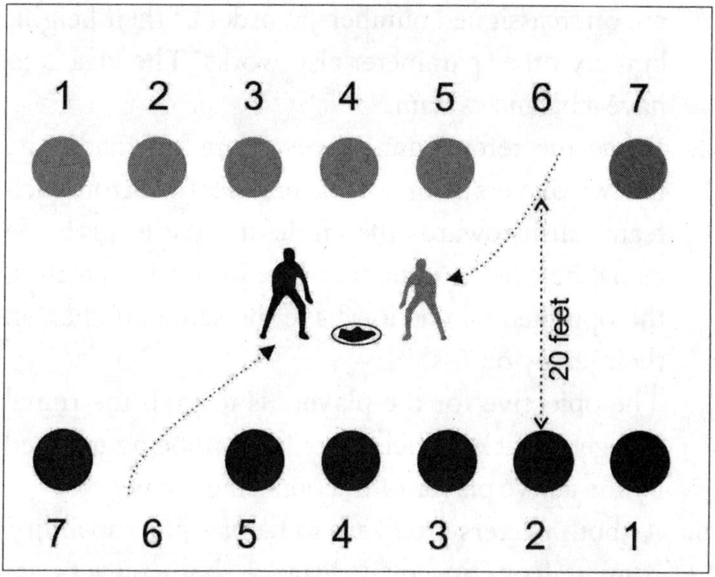

FIG. 8.2. Configuration of players just before the game begins

Playing method

1. Split the group into two teams, with one team placed on each side of the playing area along the boundary line.
2. The players of both teams stand or sit on the two lines drawn along the length of the playing area. They are about 10 ft from the circle where the rumal is placed.
3. Assign every individual on each team a number so that they are partnered with a player of the corresponding number on the opposite team. For example, if both the teams consist of eight players, then each team member is assigned the numbers from one to eight. The rumal is kept in a circle drawn in the centre of both the teams. The players

are often assigned numbers in order of their height, but any other parameter also works. The idea is to have a balanced team.

4. When the referee announces a number randomly, the two players assigned that number (one from each team) rush towards the circle and try to grab the rumal before the opponent can. In official matches, the opponents in action have the same number on their jersey or T-shirt.
5. The objective for the players is to grab the rumal and get it back to their team without being touched by the active player of the opposing team.
6. As both players are likely to be of equal capability, coming from an equal distance, both players are likely to arrive together near the rumal. They hover near the rumal and wait for the right opportunity to pick it.
7. If one of the players picks up the rumal, the other player attempts to snatch it from the opponent. If the opponent touches the rumal, then the play ends for this round. The opponent will be given the rumal, and he or she returns home the winner with a gain of three points.
8. Even if a player has first picked the rumal, the opponent who succeeds in touching it still gains the point.
9. If a player picks the rumal and finds the opponent close enough to touch it as he or she is rushing towards the home side, then the player can just drop the rumal at that place. He or she gets no points, but the opponent who now freely picks up the rumal and takes it to their home gets one point.

10. The player who first picks and returns home without the opponent touching the rumal gets three points.

Scoring

1. If players return to their team with the rumal without being touched by the opponent, the team gets three points.
2. If players are touched by the opponent but still escape, rush and bring the rumal to their side, the team gets one point.
3. If players grab the rumal but are stopped by the opponent and the opponent snatches the rumal, then the opponents get one point.
4. The team's total score is an aggregate of points scored by each player of that team, and the team that scores the most points in total wins.

Rules

1. From each team, only one player comes to grab the rumal.
2. No player at any time can touch the opponent. They can only touch the rumal or the fist in case the rumal is inside it.
3. Players must have the handkerchief in their hands to win points.
4. The game is over when all the players have been called out to play.

Positions, tasks and techniques

TABLE 8.2

Roles	*Positions*	*Tasks*	*Strategy | Techniques*
The active player	Sit in the assigned positions until the player's number is called out.	Race towards the centre the moment the number is announced to beat the opponent, with maximum speed and attention. Once the rumal is grabbed, quickly rush to the assigned side before the opponent can touch the rumal.	Pay attention to the announcement of the number, and be ready to rush. Keep the balance to turn around and slip away after picking up the rumal.
Other members	Sit in the assigned positions.	Listen carefully if their number is announced. The moment their number is announced, they take on the role of the active player. Cheer while their team member is on the run.	Stay in a running position, like athletes just before a race. Tighten muscles with preparedness.

Key skills required

Dexterity, feinting, agility and quick reactions, along with concentration and focused orientation, are the key skills to win through the rare chances of the opponent's distraction. Pretending to snatch and trying various moves with sudden shifts in direction helps in winning.

This is an outdoor game but can be played indoors too. It is played as a quick recreational activity in birthday parties, kitty parties or corporate group outings. Any individual with quick reflex actions and concentration can win.

Caution

The players in both teams who are not active should stand in a row and observe the play. They should not distract or obstruct the active players by rushing near the centre. Doing so can create confusion, and players may fall.

Skills developed

The players learn to form balanced teams dividing all the weak and strong players equally into two groups. The game helps players develop observation skills as they try to figure out the best approach to get the rumal to their side. The players learn to cheer their team members and be supportive team players.

Life lessons

Achievements are an important aspect of everyone's life. Grabbing the rumal after much struggle and bringing it to the team boosts the player's self-confidence. Children also learn to play an individual role even though the whole team is present and cheering. The cheering attitude and encouraging language of other members promote empathy and social awareness, which builds good rapport among the players.

Current state

Wrestlers of national and international repute from Haryana, Punjab, Rajasthan, Uttar Pradesh, Delhi and other Indian states participate in the game in different state events.

A first-hand experience of ancient and traditional celebrations, the Matsya festival held in Alwar in Rajasthan, India, encourages locals and tourists across the world to be a part of this game. This multi-day fiesta honours and celebrates the rich social culture, legacy and history of the region, and rumal jhapatta is a prominent game among other traditional showcases.

Variation

The umpire can call more than one number. In that case, several players from each side rush forward to participate, but a player may only tag the opponent with whom they share their number.

Similar games

Big ball soccer: The rumal, in this case, is a big soccer ball. The rules are the same as rumal jhapatta, but the game doesn't involve any tagging of players. The players can just rush to their side with the ball without being chased by the opponent.

Tunnel rats: In this version, each team lines up in a single line facing front towards the centre. When the player's number is called, the team must spread their legs to create a tunnel. The player must then crawl like a rat through the tunnel and out and be the first person to grab the rumal.

Bandar kila: In this game, a circle is drawn on the ground, in which one player (*bandar* or monkey) is tied to a *kila* (pole). All the other players place their chappals near the pole. The bandar stays in the circle only, and all the players must steal the chappals without being caught. If the bandar touches any player while stealing the chappal, that player becomes the next bandar.

Glossary

rumal	Handkerchief or a scarf
jhapatta	Sudden snatch
cheel	Vulture

9

Jod Saakli

સાંકળ સાત્તાળી

जोड़ साखळी

Son-sakali

Chain tag

Blob

Gargon

Introduction

The game *jod saakli* (chain) is a unique form of the classic run-and-chase game. It is played by running together with linked hands and involves group moves and coordination. The game consists of a chaser whose aim is to run and catch the other players. Once the chaser catches a player, that player joins hands with the chaser, and they both now chase together. When their pair has caught the third player, then this player also gets added. The chain, now formed of three players, chases other players and so on.

Other names

TABLE 9.1

Region	*Name*	*Region*	*Name*
Maharashtra	*Jod saakli, Son sankali*	Australia, New Zealand	Gang up tiggy
Gujarat	*Sankal sattali*	United States of America, United Kingdom	Chain tag
Netherlands	*Blob, Gargon*		

The play

The game tests the stamina, coordination with the other runners and escape tricks of each player.

Number of players

The game is enjoyable with six or more players. We suggest a maximum of 12 players. The beauty of this game is that more players can join in at any stage during the game.

Playground

This game is an outdoor game that involves running and chasing. So any open ground with an even surface and without potholes—grass fields, school compounds, streets, parks—will be suitable for playing. Mark a boundary according to the number of players. An area measuring 60 ft x 60 ft will suffice for 10 players.

Equipment

No equipment or any arrangement is needed to play this game except for marking boundary lines.

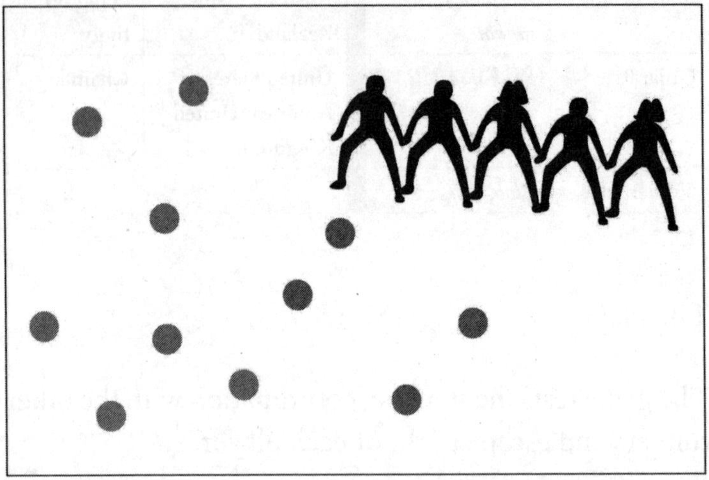

FIG. 9.1. Players in black are chasers, and the dots are runners

Playing method

Start the game by selecting a chaser. Other players in the group will be the runners.

1. All the players spread out in the playfield. On the captain's signal, the chaser starts to chase the other players and catches anyone possible.
2. After the first runner is caught, the player joins the first chaser as an integral member of the chasing team.
3. Both chasers now hold each other's hands and run together to catch the next runner.
4. As the chasers catch more runners, these runners join the chasing team. They join hands to form a

chain and chase the remaining runners together. As both the hands of the chasers are locked in the chain except for those at the end, only the two chasers at the end can tag a runner with their free hand.

5. Eventually, the chain of chasers becomes longer, and the game continues until all other players are linked in the chain except the last one.
6. The first runner to get caught gets one point, the second player to get caught gets two points, and so on. The last player gets the maximum points and wins the innings.
7. Players can choose to play more innings, and the points gained by the players in the second innings will be added to the points from the first innings. As they play more innings, the points will get added.
8. The player with the maximum points at the end of the game is declared the winner.
9. Runners are allowed to move around the playing area and have to stay away from the chain chasers.

Scoring

The score gained is based on the order in which a runner is caught. The first person to get caught gets the least points, and the points increase in the order of getting caught.

The first runner to get caught gets one point, the second two points and so on. The last player gets the maximum points. If there are nine players, then the last player standing gets eight points and is declared the winner for the innings.

Rules

1. The hands of all the chasers must be locked in the chain at all times. The players in the middle can't unlock their hands and tag runners independently.
2. If the chain is broken at the time of tagging a runner, then this tag is not valid.
3. The runners who move out of the boundary are automatically ruled out of the group and join the chain of chasers to catch the remaining players.
4. The chain must not be broken, and it goes on increasing in length as more players join.
5. The player who is caught first will be the chaser of the next game.

Positions, tasks and techniques

TABLE 9.2

Roles	*Positions*	*Tasks*	*Strategy* | *Techniques*
Chaser	Initially, take a position at any corner of the ground.	Chase and catch the runners who are spread out randomly and run in the field. Pair with the first person tagged and progressively form a chain of chasers. Make as many players as possible join the chaser's chain.	As there are many individuals in the chain with a common objective, coordination is the key. Pick one runner at a time to chase and communicate accordingly. Let all the new members take the lead from the first chaser to ensure coordination. As the length increases, running together may be difficult. So a slow run or a walk may be preferred.

Roles	*Positions*	*Tasks*	*Strategy / Techniques*
Runners	Take random positions on the ground.	Escape the chasers and keep evading. Let the chasers catch the other runners.	Run through narrow areas where the chain of chasers cannot reach. Rapidly change direction to make it difficult for chasers to follow instantly.

Variations of the game

1. In some variations, the chaser throws a ball at the targeted runner instead of touching them. The original chaser and the new joiners use the ball to tag the runners.
2. In the original game, when the chasers catch the fourth player, the chain is divided into two groups of two. The next player becomes the third member of a chain. But when the next runner is tagged, the last two players make a separate chain. So at any time, a maximum of three persons can form a chain.
3. Make a safe zone. It might be one of the sides on the playground or a tree or a bench or a space marked out with chalk. When a runner reaches this area, they are safe from being tagged. A time limit is set for staying in the safe zone.

Key skills required

1. *Coordination*: This game requires players to move while linked to other players.
2. *Communication*: Players should be able to convey and grasp the messages about the next activity without using verbal interaction.

This game can be played by any individual of age six to eighteen years. The senior players also enjoy this game with people of the same age group. Any player who is an average runner and knows the tag games can enjoy the game.

Skills developed

Children learn skills like running, evading, cooperating and being inclusive in a group setting. They learn to accept and follow the decisions of the group or the leader. Uniquely, in this game, the players learn to manage their personal feeling of enthusiasm and eagerness in accordance with the group decision. The game enhances coordination and team spirit, especially in children.

Cautions

While moving together in a chain, the chasers should be careful to maintain the same running speed as the group so as not to stumble or fall. The stronger chasers in the chain should be careful not to pull their partners too hard, forcing them to match their speed.

Life lessons

The game conveys a message of teamwork. The chasers can spread out in a larger area as a chain and can quickly catch the runners.

At the same time, there is a negative side—the 'excessive resource' problems. Many groups, families or organisations that grow large are unable to align individual resources towards a joint objective. Many individuals often pull in opposite directions, dragging down the entire organisation. So the variation of the game where the chain is broken into smaller chains provides better management.

Current state

The game is still popular as a favourite pastime in school recesses as it can be played without any planning.

Similar games

Region	*Name*
Western countries	Reverse tag/Zombi tag
Romania	*Leapsa*
Modern Greece	*Kynigito*

Glossary

saakli	Chain: Chasers link hands and move together to catch the runners
jod	Linkage or a connect
sankal sattali	'Seven claps forming a chain', referring to seven chasers joining hands to form a chain
son saakli	Golden chain

10

Vish Amrut

बर्फ पानी
Freeze tag
Lock and key
Ice and water
Stuck in the mud

Introduction

Vish amrut is the original name of the popular chasing game that has recently come to be known as 'lock and key'. With unique features, the play involves lots of running and group cooperation. The terms *vish* (poison) and *amrut*[1] (elixir) are used as symbols for suspending the players out of the game and making them active in the play again, respectively. In this form, the chaser tags and suspends the runners from the play, and the runner's teammates revive them by touching them.

The game is played in villages and small towns all over India, especially in Andhra Pradesh, Tamil Nadu, Punjab and Gujarat, and in other countries, including Pakistan, Cambodia and Italy.

[1] Also pronounced as amrit.

Other names

TABLE 10.1

Region	Name	Region	Name
Tamil Nadu	*Uyir eluppu*	United States	Freeze tag
India	*Barf-paani* or ice and water, lock and key	United Kingdom	Stuck in the mud

The play

This tag game doesn't require any arrangements except a plain bounded play area. This game involves the complexity of playing a double role at a time—reviving frozen mates by unfreezing them and saving oneself from getting tagged out by the chaser.

FIG. 10.1. A runner giving amrut to the frozen teammate

Playing method

1. One player is selected as the chaser—either voluntarily or by writing everyone's names on pieces of paper and choosing one. Chasers stay in one corner of the playfield.
2. Other players are distributed across the field randomly.
3. The chaser will chase other players to give them vish by touching them and loudly saying 'vish'.
4. As soon as vish is given to a player, this player stays still as a statue and cannot move.
5. Other players attempt to touch the player frozen with vish to set him or her free, and the moment a player succeeds, he or she shouts 'amrut'. Now, the player with vish has been revived, and he or she too joins other players.
6. The chaser continues to touch other players and give vish to make them a statue and suspend them from the play. The mission of the chaser is to freeze all the players.
7. Any player without vish can give amrut to the frozen players. The game continues as the chaser keeps giving vish and other players keep giving amrut.
8. The game ends when all players have been given vish except the last runner, and no one is left to give amrut.
9. The time taken by the chaser to complete the game is the score.
10. The next game starts with another chaser, generally the person who has been given vish the maximum number of times.

11. In fixed-time format, the players can set rules for ending the chaser's turn by setting a time limit or when any player has been given vish three times. The player who is given vish three times will be the next chaser.

Scoring

1. The runner who gives amrut and successfully revives a teammate without being caught by the chaser gets one point for each time amrut is given.
2. If any player is given vish three times, then he or she is immediately removed from the game.
3. In the end, the player who has scored the most points wins that round.

Rules

1. Upon catching any runner, the chaser must loudly say 'vish'.
2. Once the chaser touches a player and gives vish, that player is temporarily suspended from the game.
3. The chaser and other players are not allowed to go out of the restricted area while playing.
4. A player, while giving amrut, may not be given vish. The chaser cannot stand around waiting for them to finish and should be at least 4 ft away from the frozen runners.
5. The runners must loudly say 'amrut' while touching and unfreezing their teammates.

Positions, tasks and techniques

TABLE 10.2

Roles	*Positions*	*Tasks*	*Strategy | Techniques*
Chaser	Stand in any one of the corners, ready to enter the playfield.	Chase the runners and suspend them from the game by giving vish by touching them.	Target the weaker player first and try to catch the runners who go closer to the frozen player—the trick is in deciding whether to prevent the suspended player from getting amrut or catch other players who are still active.
Runners	Randomly spread out on the ground away from the chaser.	Escape the chaser's touch and outlast other runners. Unfreeze the teammates by touching and giving them amrut.	One or more players can distract the chaser so the other runners can give amrut. Make swift movements to confuse the chaser

Key skills required

This run-and-chase game requires running fast, being alert and keen observation of the movement of the others.

Children of the age group five to fifteen years love this game. Considering that no specific skills are required, people of mixed age groups can enjoy it together. It can be played in short school recesses or as a vacation street game.

Caution

Hard contact or aggressive pushes to give vish or amrut might cause the person to fall on the ground. Also, the touch to give amrut to teammates should be a gentle touch or a light tap on the shoulder.

Skills developed

This fun game provides children with a platform to socialise and interact with children of mixed age groups. Playing this game helps players to build up their physical strength while developing their sense of distance and space. Individual participation and cooperation to safeguard mates is the unique feature of this game.

Variation

The chaser can designate particular styles of moves to the other players. For example, instead of running, the runners can be made to hop, walk or skip throughout the game. For the runners, one can add a unique style to give amrut, for example, shaking hands instead of just touching.

Life lessons

This game gives confidence to children to depend on others to save them. Further, it teaches them to cooperate with others and help them in difficult times. It spread a positive message that the effect of vish (negatives) can be defeated by amrut (good deeds).

Current state

In townships and villages, this game is still popular among school children. They play in recess or around their homes. The game, however, is not given much importance as a team sport in the physical training curriculum.

Origin and references

Samudra manthan and the concept of confrontation of duality—good and bad, dark and light—exist in our culture. The game is believed to have been derived from *Deva* and *Danav* qualities and the belief that communities can be saved by inducing positive forces in the form of amrut.

Similar games

Hot dog tag (United States of America)

This is an interesting deviation from the classic vish amrut. When the chaser touches a runner, the runner must lie flat on the floor with hands by their side and legs together as a 'hot dog'. For the tagged player to get back into the game, two free players need to lie on either side of the hot dog to form the buns. The chaser cannot tag any of the three players completing the hot dog, as they are allowed to join back in.

Shadows (Ireland)

The chaser must stand in the runner's shadows to catch them. If you are being chased, you can run to a shaded place where you have no shadow, and then you are safe. So there would be a constant search for shaded areas. This game is played during the daytime for the requirement of sunlight that forms shadows.

Glossary

To give Vish	To suspend the runner from the game by touching
To give Amrut	To revive the suspended teammate by touching
To freeze	Make the runner still at one place

11

Kho-kho

रथेरा

खो-ध्वनि क्रीड़ा

छुइयाछुइयन

Game of chase

Introduction

Kho-kho is a popular form of the run-chase sport from ancient India, often a major part of the games period in schools. The game involves chasing and touching runners while running in a linear path around two poles. Techniques like forming a relay of chasers while passing on the chasing turn are used.

There are two types of kho-kho.

1. *Standing kho-kho*: One player is selected as a chaser. The other players—the runners—will be standing in pairs, one behind the other, forming a circle. The runners can run in and around the circle within a marked boundary. The runners pass on the running turn by stopping and standing in front of any pair of their choice, and instantly, the player who is

standing behind in the pair becomes the new runner. This type of kho-kho is a relay of runners.

2. *Sitting kho-kho*: This type is played by forming a relay of chasers to catch the runners. This is the format described here.

Other names

In ancient times, a version of kho-kho was played on *raths* (chariots) in Maharashtra, hence the name, *rathera*.

Region	*Name*	*Region*	*Name*
Ancient India	*Kho-dhwani krida*	Maharashtra	*Rathera*
English	Game of chase	Bangladesh	*Chhoyan-chhuyin*

The play

The goal of the game is to chase and catch. Kho is a voice signal sent to communicate to other players that it is their turn to chase. The capstone of the game is strategically building a chain to catch the runner. The runners run zigzag, crossing between the sitting players, and change directions rapidly to make it tough to be tagged themselves.

Playground

The game is played on an evenly surfaced rectangular field outdoors, measuring 29 m in length and 16 m in width.

At each end of the longer side of the field, there is a free zone rectangle measuring 16 m in length and 1.50 m in width.

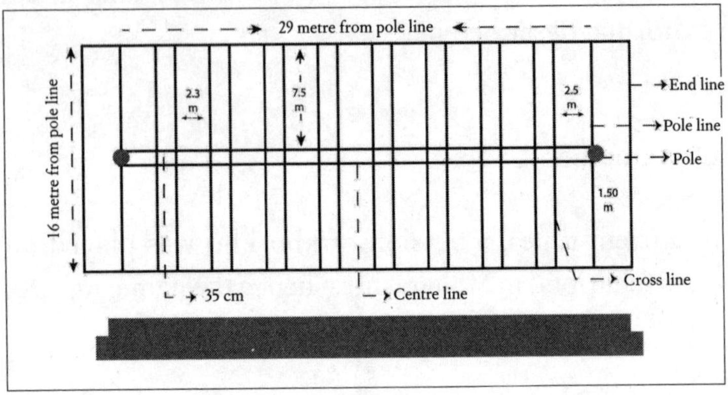

FIG. 11.1. The playfield

A centre lane 27 m long and 35 cm wide is drawn exactly from the middle of the shorter dimension of the playground. Two strong wooden poles, each 1.2 m in height and of diameter about 10 cm, are firmly fixed at both ends of the centre lane. The top of the poles is flat with smooth edges.

Eight parallel cross tracks of 30 cm width is drawn between these two wooden poles. The cross track is 2.30 m away from the next track, and a block is created in between. The intersections of the centre lane and the cross tracks form eight boxes measuring 35 cm x 30 cm each.

The eight players of the chaser team will occupy one box each to take the position of chasing.

Equipment

The required items are two poles, two watches, one whistle, one measuring tape, lime powder and score sheets for noting results.

Dress code

Informal play has no dress code. Numbered T-shirts should be worn in formal matches.

Number of players and key roles

Each kho-kho team consists of twelve players, but during a match, only nine players and a captain from each team can enter the field. In casual games, each team's captain is on the field but doesn't play. He or she keeps score and checks the fouls.

For official matches, the team also has two umpires, one timekeeper, one referee and one scorekeeper.

Play duration

A match consists of two innings. In each inning, each team gets 9 minutes for chasing and 9 minutes for defending. For official matches, the time is now reduced to 7 minutes for each innings. There is an interval of 5 minutes at the end of the innings and of 2 minutes between the turns.

FIG. 11.2. The game in progress

Playing method

Two teams face each other in this game (runners and chasers).

The game starts with a toss between the two team captains. The winning captain decides who will chase first.

1. Nine players from the chaser team enter the field. From them, eight players will sit/kneel in a row, alternating in the direction they face (adjacent members facing opposite directions) in eight boxes drawn in the central lane of the field.
2. The ninth member is the active chaser, who stands at either side of the poles, ready to start the play. The chaser in action tags out a runner by touching that player with the palm. Chasers move in the direction of the cross line to catch runners.
3. From the runner's team, a batch of three players enters the kho-kho ground at a time. After the third runner leaves the field, the next three must immediately enter the field.

4. The runners put in all their efforts to play out the 9 minutes, avoiding being touched by the chasers while not crossing the field boundaries.
5. The chaser on the move gives kho (a tap on the back and shout of 'kho') as an indication to take over the chasing turn to any teammate sitting crouched in one of the boxes in the central lane. Rapidly, that teammate gets up and rushes to catch the runners.
6. Hence, the chase or pursuit forms a series of khos, and the play continues as a relay of chasers.
7. The position of the sitting players is dynamic; one will never find the same sequence of players sitting in the same order as when the game had started.

FIG. 11.3. A Chaser's dive to catch the runner

Scoring

1. Whenever any chaser catches any of the three runners, the chaser's team gets one point.

2. If the chaser team's score is nine points more than the runners in the first innings, then the chasers can choose to take the role of runners without waiting for the next innings.
3. The team that scores the maximum points at the end of the game will be declared the winner.
4. If the match ends with a tie, a tiebreaker is played. The team that scores first is declared the winner of the match.

Rules

Rules for chasers

1. Chasers can run only in the direction which they face, and they cannot turn back. They can take a U-turn only after reaching the pole. However, according to new rules, chasers are allowed to move in the direction of their shoulder line(sideways) too.
2. The chasers are not allowed to cross the central lane drawn between the two poles. That is, they cannot pass between the sitting teammates.

> The way a team plays as a whole determines its success. You may have the greatest bunch of individual stars in the world, but if they don't play together, the club won't be worth a dime.
>
> —Babe Ruth

3. While giving kho to another chaser, the tap on the back and uttering kho loudly should be simultaneous. Any gap is considered a foul.
4. The runner will not be declared out if the sitting chaser touches him or her from the block without receiving a kho (that will be the foul of early get-up).
5. The chasers can change the running direction only after going in the free zone, beyond the poles.
6. After touching a runner, even if the chaser changes the direction (except in the free zone) before giving a kho, the runner will be considered not out.

Rules for runners

1. Runners can move anywhere in the field. They can cross the central lines without restrictions and can go between two players. They are not allowed to go outside the boundary.
2. Each team consists of twelve players, but only nine players play in a batch of three in one innings.
3. After the third and last runner of the batch is out, the next batch must enter the playfield before a kho is given by the active chaser.

Runners are declared out if:

1. they are touched by the active chaser,
2. they drift out of the playfield or
3. they enter the playfield late.

Positions, tasks and techniques

TABLE 11.1

Roles	*Positions*	*Tasks*	*Strategy | Techniques*
Chasers	Sit in the boxes, adjacent players alternatively facing the opposite direction. (One chaser stands near the pole to start the chase.)	Chase and catch the runners. Pass on the kho to the teammates nearest to any of the three runners.	Gauge the direction of the runner's moves beforehand and keep giving kho frequently to different teammates to make the chase swift and to get the runners tired soon.
Runners	Enter the field in a batch of three at a time.	Run and escape from being tagged out by the chasers who are rapidly coming one by one as a relay.	Go around the two poles and between the sitting players, making a non-linear path. Switch directions quickly to avoid getting caught. As there are nine possible chasers who can spring from their sitting position, watch their subtle movements and changes in facial expressions to predict who might start chasing.

Key skills required

Apart from the basic skills of running and chasing, players need motor skills, such as endurance, speed, agility and flexibility. They need to be responsive, cooperative and attentive to the actions of their teammates.

Some exclusive skills required include diving and dodging—both requiring agility and strength.

Kho-kho is often misconstrued as a game for children. It happens to be a universal sport enjoyed by people of all ages. Any player who can focus and run swiftly can play the game well.

Caution

While giving a kho, chasers must not push the sitting players. A sudden jerk can make them fall as they would be in a half-sitting position, ready to run at once. The runners should be careful not to stumble upon the sitting players while passing between the adjacent boxes.

Skills developed

Kho-kho is based on the natural principles of physical development. It helps to build physical fitness, strength, speed and stamina. It also helps to develop qualities such as obedience, discipline and loyalty between team members. It improves quick thinking, decision-making and swiftness in actions. It encourages players to manoeuvre, strategise and win the game. This game can be a personal development tool for the athlete to prepare themselves for other sports.

Life lessons

Players learn to be expeditious. The major learning is to analyse the moves, direction and positions of the opposite team and smartly find a way to reach the end.

Origin

Kho-kho is an ancient Indian game, possibly derived from the different strategies and tactics of the war in Kurukshetra as described in the Mahabharata. The chariot fight during the war and the zigzag pathways followed by the retreating soldiers show similarity with kho-kho. On the 11th day of the war, the chief of the *Kaurava* army, Guru Dronacharya, drew a typical strategic circular formation—the *chakravyuh*. This method, which Abhimanyu adopted, resembles the idea of ring play, a defence tactic in kho-kho.

Kho-kho was regularly played all over India, especially in Maharashtra, West Bengal, Karnataka, Madhya Pradesh, Kerala, Gujarat, Andhra Pradesh and Telangana.

Current state

In 1982, kho-kho was included as a game in the list of eligible games by the Indian Olympic Association. This game is managed by the Kho-Kho Federation of India (KKFI), established in 1956.[1]

[1] http://khokhofederation.in/

Kho-kho entered the international arena in 1987 when the Asian Kho-Kho Federation came into being. In 1993, kho-kho turned commercial. The countries that play kho-kho include Bangladesh, Sri Lanka, Maldives, Japan, Nepal, Thailand and England.

The modern rules of the game were framed at the beginning of the 20th century. Kho-kho was first demonstrated overseas in 1936 at the Berlin Olympics as a special feature by a single team. The demonstration was done before Adolf Hitler by the Hanuman Wyayam Prasarak Mandal from Amravati in Maharashtra, India.

Domestic seasons and tournaments

KKFI has its branches in all Indian states, and it conducts mini, junior and open national championships for both men and women. India is also getting an eight-city kho-kho league.[2]

Players of kho-kho are also eligible for the following awards: Arjuna, Eklavya, Rani Laxmi Bai, Veer Abhimanyu and Janaki Awards.

Variations of the game

To make the game faster and entertaining, and to bring in more official gameplay, the organisers of the franchise-based kho-kho league have changed a few rules.[3]

[2] India is getting an eight-city kho-kho league: Pune, Bengaluru confirmed.

[3] Ultimate kho-kho: Organisers tweak rules to make the sport more 'modern' and 'exciting'.

1. The duration of play has been reduced to 7 minutes from 9.
2. The points system has been restructured, and the concept of 'wazir' as a trump card to win more points was introduced.
3. More points were awarded for acrobatic catches, like after a dive or a long slip.

As per the new rules, the play will be for 28 minutes and should see more points scored.

Glossary

cross lane	Eight parallel trenches that cut the centre lane in the playfield
central lane	Lane formed by two parallel lines from one pole to the other
to give a kho	The word *kho* is uttered by an active Chaser for the other sitting teammate to pass on the chasing turn
late kho	When an active chaser delays the touch that gives kho to another
line cut	When the chaser cuts the square boxes, cross lanes or centre lane while chasing the opponent
early get up	When the chaser gets up before properly getting kho from a teammate
box	Square formed by the intersection of the centre lane and cross lanes, where each chaser takes a position
lobby	Free space around the playfield

free zone	Area of approximately 1.5 m after each pole in which the direction rule is not followed and a runner can change the direction
pole	Specially made wooden rod firmly erected at both sides of the playfield
end line	Lines running parallel to each other and equal to the width of the kho-kho field are known as end lines. The measurement of end lines is 16 m

12

Langdi

लंगड़ी टांग

நொண்டி ஆட்டம்

લંગડી

ಕುಂಟಾಟ

ଛୁଟା ଗୁଡେ଼ା

Hopscotch

Introduction

Langdi is one of the first team sports that a child in India plays in school. A chaser hops on one leg while the other leg is kept folded in the air and chases other players who keep moving to avoid getting caught.

The term langdi means to limp or to hop on one foot. This foundational field sport is useful in training for games like kho-kho, volleyball, football and gymnastics.

Other names

Table 12.1

Region	*Name*	*Region*	*Name*
North-eastern states	*Kukuraju, Aroni, Gamosa*	Punjab	*Langda sher*
Karnataka	*Kuntata*	Delhi	*Langdi tang*
Odisha	*Chuta gudo*	Gujarat	*Langdi*
Tamil Nadu	*Nondi attam*	United Kingdom, United States of America	Hopscotch

The play

The game is played by two teams, chasers and defenders. The chasers send one player at a time to the field to catch as many runners as possible while hopping on one foot. The defenders send three players at first. After all the three players are tagged out, the next batch of three runners enters the game. The team that tags the most opponents in the given time period wins the match.

Number of players

Any number of players divided into two equal teams can play informally. We recommend a minimum of six players each and that captainship be assigned to one player from each team.

For informal play, the captains of both the teams keep score records and perform the role of referees.

For official matches, there are two teams with fifteen players per team, twelve active players and three extra players. There are also two umpires, one referee, one timekeeper and two scorekeepers.

Equipment needed

Chalks or lime powder to mark boundaries, a stopwatch to check time duration and a whistle to announce turn or innings change and to declare fouls are needed.

The playground

The ground is 15 m x 15 m, and the langdi court is a square with sides of length 10 m each, marked as square ABCD. The chaser's entry zone is outside the field on the left, marked WXYZ, and the runner's entry zone is on the opposite side near the corner, marked MNOP.

The line dividing the court into two equal rectangular halves is the central line: EF. The rectangle near the chaser's entry zone is Field 1: ADFE. The other half-court near the defenders' entry zone is Field 2: EBCF.

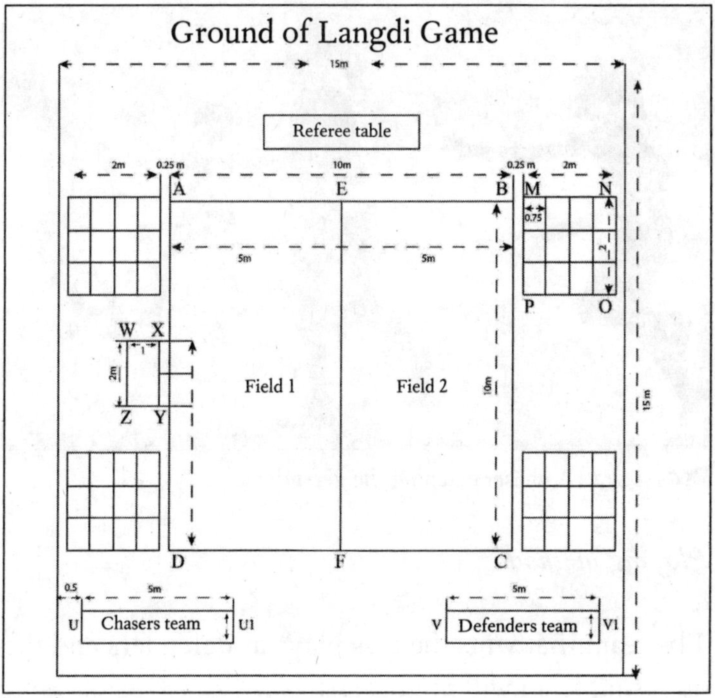

FIG. 12.1. The langdi field

The players wear T-shirts/banyans and half pants. They usually play without shoes or are allowed to wear flat-bottomed canvas shoes. On a wooden ground indoors, players should wear lightweight sports shoes.

For official matches, T-shirts are numbered in the front and back.

Play duration

Each match has two innings. Each innings involves chasing and defending turns, lasting for 9 minutes.

There is an interval of 5 minutes after an inning and a 2-minute break between turns.

FIG. 12.2. A chaser catching the defenders

Playing method

The team that wins the toss plays as defenders and the opposing team will be chasers.

1. At the start, the defenders send three players into the field. These defenders enter the field from the entry zone. Only after these three defenders are out, the next set of three defenders can enter.
2. The chasing team sends a chaser who hops on one foot and tries to tag the three defenders present on the field. The captain of the chasing team decides the sequence of the players performing langdi before the round starts. A new chaser enters the field one by one to chase after the existing chaser is out.
3. Defenders are declared out if the chaser touches them with the palm. Any defender who steps out of the ground is also out.
4. When all the chasers are out, then the turn for the chasers is over. The score is calculated based on the number of defenders tagged out.

5. The end of the allotted time also ends the turn.
6. The team that catches most defenders n gets a higher score and is declared the winner.
7. Generally, only one match at a time is played as this play is strenuous for legs.

Rules

1. Except for the chaser on the move, no other chaser shall enter the field. The next chaser will enter the field only after the previous chaser has left.
2. Defenders must not disturb or obstruct the chasers, or else they will be declared out.
3. When a chaser touches a defender with his or her palm, the defender will be declared out.
4. Other than the touch with the palm, no touch is valid for declaring the defender out.
5. After the first batch of three defenders is ruled out, the new batch of three defenders enter the field immediately from the entry zone. These three players must enter together.
6. If all the defenders are tagged out before the chaser's turn is over, the defenders play again and maintain the same order of entering the field. The order of the defenders entering the court will not be changed during a turn.
7. After the completion of the first innings, if the points of the chasers exceed the points of their opponents by nine or more, then the chasers will have the option of again taking their turn as chasers.
8. If a match is not completed for any reason, it will be continued at another time with the same players and

the same captain. It resumes from the unfinished turn, and the teams start off with the scores from the earlier play.

Scoring

1. The chasing team scores one point each for any defender declared out.
2. If there is a tie, one more inning (one turn for both the teams as chasers and defenders) will be played. Before starting the tiebreaker innings, a break of 5 minutes is to be given.
3. Alternatively, a quick tiebreaker innings is also played on a minimum chase basis. As soon as the first point is scored, the turn will be declared over, and the time taken for the scoring of this first point is recorded for both teams. The team that took less time to score this point will be declared the winner of the match.

Positions, tasks and techniques

TABLE 12.2

Roles	*Positions*	*Tasks*	*Strategy / Techniques*
Chaser	Take a position at the chaser's entry zone marked along the boundary of the field.	Chase the defenders by hopping on one foot to tag them out.	Take long steps to avoid stress on the knees while hopping on one leg. Change the direction of moves rapidly to catch less attentive defenders.

Roles	*Positions*	*Tasks*	*Strategy | Techniques*
Defenders	Enter the court from the defender team's entry zone in a batch of three players.	Run and escape the chaser's touch, and stay in the court as long as possible.	Shift rapidly in different directions, and dodge to mislead the chaser.
Chasers' captain	Stand at an appropriate place from where the game can be observed well. Choose to perform at any point.	Decide the sequence of players to perform langdi and keep a note of the number of tagged out defenders. Maintain the score sheet.	Wisely select the opening set of chasers to perform, to tag out the maximum number of defenders as early as possible. Sending weaker performers at the start boosts the opponent's confidence.
Runners' captain	Watch from outside in the beginning. Go as the last player.	Identify the first batch of three players and plan the next batches to enter the field. Maintain the score sheet.	Select the fastest three players in the first batch so as to extend the play as much as possible.

Key skills required

While chasing, players should be skilled enough to balance on one foot while hopping. They must not lose balance and yet run with speed. The runners should be swift and agile to escape the chasers.

Langdi can be played extempore as it requires little arrangement and can be played by anyone irrespective of age and gender. The players just have to hop on one foot, so any individual with average hopping speed can participate. It can be a great family gathering game between the different age groups.

Balancing on one foot is tough for many individuals, and they may find this game challenging.

Caution

The ground should be of a comfortable temperature. During summer, the ground becomes hot, especially during the day, and could hurt the feet of the players as the game is played barefoot.

Skills developed

Playing langdi strengthens leg muscles and improves the stability of movements. Along with physical ability, it enhances swift reflexes, concentration, alertness and energy levels.

There is an effort to popularise this game amongst young footballers in Germany as a base game.

Life lessons

This basic game teaches children to enjoy playing without any complex rules and tough competitions that involve do-or-die situations. Players learn through this large group game that even unskilful, weaker or untrained participants can play roles in forming a team to sustain through the given timeline.

Current state

Langdi is now professionally played in clubs after the formation of the Langadi Federation of India in 2009. Langdi made its entry into the international sports field in 2013 as a bilateral competition between Nepal and India. In 2014, the first triangular championship was conducted in Bhutan between Nepal, India and Bhutan.

The fourth National Men's and Women's Langdi Championship was held in Chandigarh, India, in May 2013. Mumbai University introduced langdi as a sport at the college level in 2014 to encourage fitness amongst its students. The first Asian Games for langdi were organised in Bangkok, Thailand, in 2015.

Variations of the game

Instead of using only one leg, some variations allow both legs, one at a time, to allow equal exercise and muscle formations for both legs. An imbalance may also cause strain in other parts of the body.

This approach has invited praise as well as criticism. Using the weaker leg also increases the risk of injury. Most people have a dominant leg, and there are many supporters of the one-leg-only format, which uses only one leg for the game. In archery, long jump and triple jumps, the players use their dominant leg.

Similar games

Nondi: As discussed in Chapter 3, Nondi also involves hopping on one leg.

Glossary

fields	Demarcated area restricting the designated players inside during the game
central line	Line that divides the ground into two halves
change of leg	When a chaser changes his or her foot and starts playing langdi on the other foot
retired	If runners leave the field of their own accord

13

Gella Chutt

सीता उद्धार

বাউচি

മണ്ഡി കുഞ്ജു

Prisoner's base

Dare base

Introduction

Gella chutt is an outdoor team game of Tripura, India, once widely popular in north-east India. Played by two groups, the king group and the enemy group, it is a form of run-and-chase game. The objective is to save the king from prison and aid that player to reach the house. The king's move from the prison to the house is called gella chutt, which translates to 'the king ran away'.

The king's group, called *rakshak*, attempts to free the king by sending a team member to the prison to rescue the king. They should avoid being captured by a member of the opposing team. The enemy group is called *shatru*. Shatru players scatter all around the prison to prevent the king's escape. The rakshaks focus on the king's moves. They save him or her from the enemy by forming a fence around the king and moving ahead quickly while tagging out the enemies.

Other names

TABLE 13.1

Region	*Name*	*Region*	*Name*
Bihar, Uttar Pradesh	*Seeta uddhar*	Punjab	*Budhi basanti*
Kerala	*Mandi kunju*	West Bengal	*Budhi kapati, bau-basanti, budir chu, bauchi*
United States of America	Dare base	Medieval Europe	Prisoner's base

The play

The game's objective is for the player of the rakshak group to take the king to the house from the circular court marked as the prison. They must pass through an area in which the opponents (enemies) are scattered to catch the king and the defenders. If the king makes it to the house, then the rakshaks earn a point. If any shatru touches the king, then the king is declared dead. The teams then interchange roles to play the next round. With a lot of players running, this game is lively and exciting at all times.

Number of players and key roles

The game is played by two teams: the king group and the enemy group. The number of players in each group is around seven to nine. The number of participants in the game may differ depending on the size of the playing area and the number of available players. From the defending group, a player—generally the strongest one—is selected as the king. This player is crucial as the play revolves around saving or catching the king.

Playground

This game requires two regions in the playground, 50 m apart. There is one rectangular region on the left and a circular one called the prison on the right. The sizes of the courts can be drawn as per the number of players in a team. Typically, the prison is about 2 m in diameter, and the house is about 5 m x 2 m. The house should accommodate all the rakshaks except the king. The external boundary of the play area is about 60 m x 30 m, but the area can be reduced or enlarged based on the availability of space and the number of players.

Equipment needed

Chalk sticks or lime powder is required to mark the boundaries of the play area.

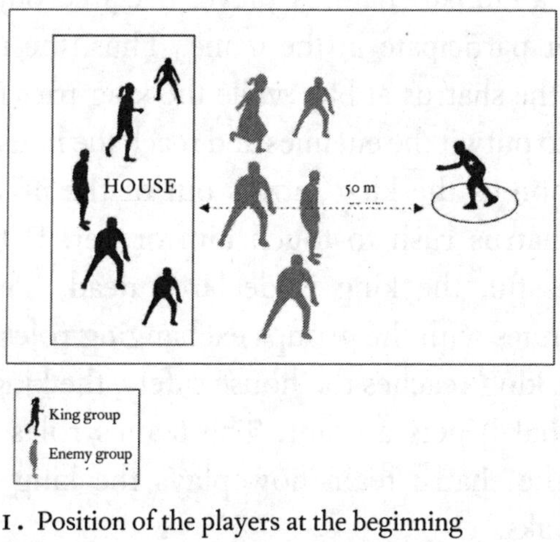

FIG. 13.1. Position of the players at the beginning

Playing method

1. From the rakshaks, one player is designated as the king. The king takes a position in the circle marked as the prison. The people stay in the house, in the large box on the left.
2. The king aims to escape from the prison and rush to the house without being touched by a shatru. The shatrus spread out to stop the king from reaching the house.
3. The game starts when the rakshaks run one by one towards the prison shouting '*kut, kut*'. The rakshak team forms a chain by joining hands to safeguard the king while he or she is escaping from prison and also to tag opponents who come in their way.
4. If a shatru is touched by a rakshak, then both the players are declared out and take no further part in the game. Therefore, both sides avoid touching each other.
5. Rakshaks are permitted to go inside the prison and make a human chain. A player declared out can no longer participate in the game. Thus, the rakshaks keep the shatrus at bay while the king tries to find a way to outwit the enemies and reach the house safely.
6. As soon as the king moves out of the prison cell, the shatrus rush to touch him or her. If they are successful, the king is declared dead. The game continues with the groups exchanging roles.
7. If the king reaches the house safely, the king's team (rakshaks) gets a point. The team's roles change, and the shatru team now plays the king and the rakshaks.

8. The rakshaks get only five chances to send the defenders for the king's rescue. After that, they lose the opportunity to save the king, and the game continues with a reversal of roles.
9. The rakshaks can score maximum 10 points at a stretch. After that, they take the role of the enemy group.

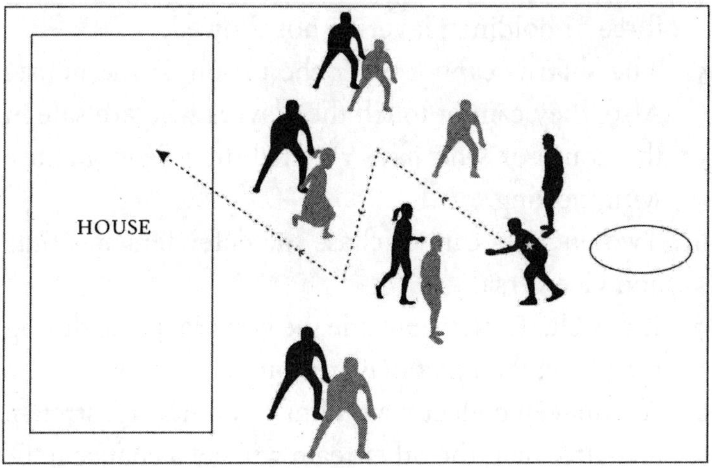

FIG. 13.2. Players in action with the king shown with a star

Rules

1. If any team member touches the opposing team members other than the king, then both members are out of the game. These players can enter the game only in the next round after the next king is selected.
2. If a shatru touches the king, then the king is considered dead, and the rakshaks lose against the

enemy. Now the enemy group plays as the king and rakshaks.

3. If rakshaks attempting to rescue the king make it through the opposing team from house to prison without being caught, they are safe while in the prison and can pick their own time to run with the king back to their side of the line.
4. Only touching with the hand is allowed. Using force or holding players is not allowed.
5. The shatrus cannot enter the prison or the house. Also, they cannot touch the players who are safe in the house or who have reached the prison and are with the king.
6. Two enemies cannot chase the defenders at a time and vice versa.
7. If any shatru steps outside the boundary line during the chase, then that player is out.
8. A team can collect maximum 10 points at a stretch, and after that, the other team will get a chance to be the rakshaks.
9. If any rakshak reaches the prison, he or she can take shelter in the prison with the king, and the king can wait for an opportunity to return to the house any time. In case the player is unable to return to the house but the king has reached, then the player is out of the game. To revive and take the player for the rest of the game, the team can sacrifice one point they collected.
10. To pause the play, the team or any player can ask the captain for a 2-minute break. During the break, the king cannot return to the house. This break cannot be taken during any chase or action.

Scoring

1. The rakshaks get two points for each time the king safely reaches the house.
2. If the enemy group touches the king, the king is considered dead. Then the enemy group will get one point.
3. The game can continue for three rounds or for a decided time. In the end, the total points of both the teams are compared to declare the winning team. In many informal games, though, no score is recorded.

Positions, tasks and techniques

TABLE 13.2

Roles	*Positions*	*Tasks*	*Strategy | Techniques*
King	Take a position in prison.	Attempt to escape the prison and reach the house with the support of the rakshaks.	Do not leave the prison until some of the teammates come to guard and support in escaping. The king is the key player, and therefore, staying alive is the primary objective while escaping.
Rakshaks	At the start, take a position in the house.	Run towards the prison, one by one, to support the king's escape and guard the king against tagging by the shatru group.	Focus on the king's moves and save him or her from the shatru by forming a fence. Move ahead quickly while tagging out the enemies.

Roles	*Positions*	*Tasks*	*Strategy | Techniques*
Shatrus	Surround the prison and scatter in the field.	Follow the rakshaks moving towards the prison, tag them out and keep a watch to instantly tag the king if he or she leaves the prison.	Try to divert the attention of the players guarding the king and separate them from the king.

Key skills required

Fast running, quick decision making and vigilance are preferred skills for the participants. The player selected as the king is at the centre of the game, so that player needs to be strong, swift and more alert to be on the winning side. The game engages the players in a series of feints and dares.

Gella chutt is ideal for a big group of players and with large open spaces as playfields. Players aged between eight to fifteen can play this game on the grounds near their houses or even on the streets. The game is running and chasing, and no specific skill or training is essential to begin playing.

Caution

The game involves speed and zigzag running, so the playground should be even-surfaced and dry to avoid any injury from stumbling.

Though unnecessary in casual games, it is advisable to draw an outer boundary of the playing area to avoid unnecessary arguments if some players run far away. You may assign some trees, buildings or a road as the end of the playground.

Skills developed

The game allows for vigorous exercise, judgement of movements and risk-taking. It develops the running speed of players, logical thinking and cooperative strategy-building.

Life lessons

The game develops decision-making ability, keeping the team objective as the primary goal. The players may be in a dilemma because they have to choose between self-safety and common interest. At times, in the game, if they choose to act in self-interest, it may push the team to a loss. We sometimes face this situation in the course of life, and the experience gained in the game can be helpful to make the right decisions. An article on the website PsycholoGenie furnishes the meaning of this concept along with examples.[1]

[1] https://psychologenie.com/meaning-of-prisoners-dilemma-with-real-life-examples

Current state

The game has lost its popularity in India now. In the villages of Tripura and Uttar Pradesh, however, we may find children enjoying this game.

The game is also known as dare base in Western countries. In F. Anstey's comic novel *Vice Versa* (1882), the boys at Dr Grimstone's boarding school are required to play a game called 'chevy' and said to be commonly known as a prisoners' base.

Dare Base was the original title of the 1952 Nero Wolfe mystery novel *Prisoner's Base* by Rex Stout (1886–1975). The plot clearly references the game.

Variations of the game

Budi basanti or Seeta uddhaar /bauchi (The old lady)

Instead of the king in prison, the key player is Seeta, who is captured and kept in Lanka and guarded by demons. The other players of the team are in the big circle, and their goal is to rescue Seeta from captivity, just like we discussed rescuing the king. The chief variation is the rakshaks hold their breath when they go to Lanka and come back to Ayodhya, like in kabaddi.

Glossary

gella	King
chutt	Ran away/escaped

14

Atya-patya

सारागरी

ખારો પાટ

கிளித்தட்டு

आटयापाटया

দৰিয়া বান্ধা

Introduction

Fairly popular in Maharashtra and Tamil Nadu, *atya-patya* is an ancient athletic sport with complex rules. Known as *kilithattu* in Tamil Nadu, the game has long been marked as a test of strategic thinking and physical agility. This game promotes Tamil identity on a national platform.

The play involves running to the end of the playfield and back, cutting nine breadthwise sections while defending against the opposing team's efforts to obstruct. Besides entertainment and exercise, the sport is a fine combination of individual swiftness and collective team performance.

Other names

TABLE 14.1

Region	Name	Region	Name
Gujarat	*Aata-pata, Kharo-paat, Luni -paat*	Maharashtra	*Sur-patya, Atya-patya, Saragari, Saramani*
Tamil Nadu	*Kilithattu, Thattukada, Uppukodu, Uppupattai*	Punjab	*Lonapati, Surpati chikka*
Bengal	*Doria bandha*	Europe	Game of feints, Militant chase

The play

The goal of the offensive team is to cross all the trenches and return to the front trench to score points. If any of the offensive team players succeed in moving across all the sections and return safely, without being touched by any of the opposing team members minding the trenches, the offensive team earns the full score. The team on offence is called *lonawale*, and the defenders are *patiwale*.

FIG. 14.1. Two teams, lonawale (in grey) and patiwale (in black)

Equipment needed

A chalk powder or white powder to draw the baselines, a whistle, a stopwatch and score sheets are needed.

There is no dress code for informal games. The game is played barefoot for both informal and official matches. The players wear shorts and numbered T-shirts, having different colours for each team in official matches.

Playground

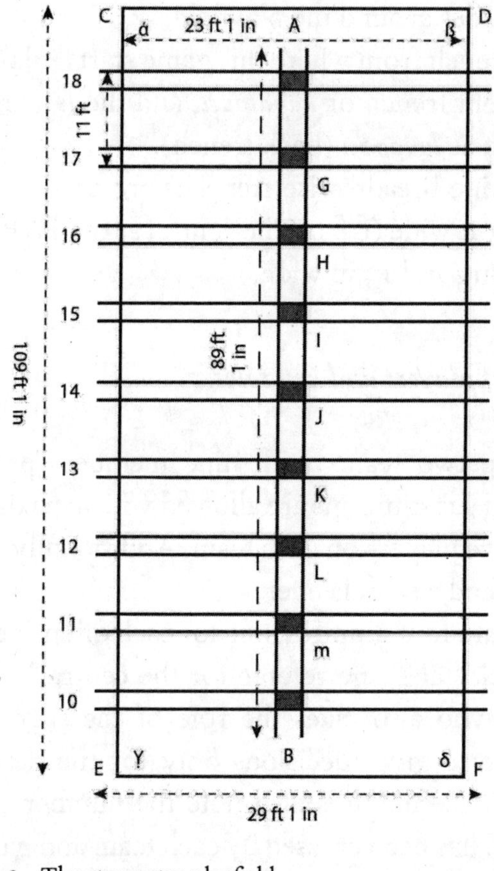

FIG. 14.2. The atya-patya playfield

1. The playfield for atya-patya is marked with lines measuring 109 ft 1 in long (CE and DF in the diagram) and 29 ft 1 in wide (CD and EF).
2. The playground consists of eight rectangles created by drawing one vertical and nine horizontal trenches. The lengthwise trench that divides all trenches horizontally into halves is the central trench or *surpati*. The player who guards the surpati (the trench) and prevents the opponents from crossing is called *surr*. There will be a clear space of 10 ft from both upper and lower sides and 3 ft from the left and right sides around the playfield.
3. The trench from where this game starts is known as the front trench or *kapalpati*, and the last trench is known as *lonapati* (back trench).
4. The nine breadthwise trenches are 23 ft 1 in long and 13 ft wide ($\alpha\beta$). The central surpati AB is 89 ft 1 in long and 13 in wide.

Number of players and key roles

There are two teams with nine members per team. Unlimited substitutions are allowed with a maximum of two reserve players on each team. Additionally, there is a referee and a scorekeeper.

There are four umpires, one for each offensive player on the field, and one referee for the central and front trenches who also takes the role of the surr empire. Each umpire gives decisions only for the designated trench. These umpires also note the number of times the trench has been crossed by each team and hand over the records to the referee and the scorekeeper at the end of the game.

Time duration

Each game consists of two innings. At the end of each inning, there is a break of 5 minutes. Each team gets 7 minutes of playtime with a 2-minute break in between. The final result is decided based on the results of three matches.

FIG. 14.3. The surr and the patiwala obstructing lonawala members

Playing method[1]

The game is played by two teams: the patiwale (defenders) and the lonawale (raiders). The individual members are referred to as patiwala and lonawala.

1 https://www.youtube.com/watch?v=hiHhMukoyx4

The goal for the patiwale is to obstruct the lonawale when they proceed through each track. The patiwale stand in each square at the intersection. At first, a batch of four members of the lonawale team enter the field and have to race to the next rectangular sections (between the trenches), dodging the patiwale.

1. A coin toss decides which team plays as lonawale or patiwale. The referee starts the game by blowing a whistle.
2. Eight players from the patiwale team take their positions in each intersection formed by a trench and the surpati, one on each intersection facing the front trench. (Each of the trenches, excluding the front trench, is consecutively labelled as the first, second, ... up to the last one, eighth.)
3. The patiwale stand in trenches to obstruct the lonawale players by tagging them out, thus preventing them from returning to the front trench after reaching the back trench. A successful return is called scoring a *lona*.
4. The surr (the lead) will stand at the front of the surpati, ready to cut the squares (to rush up to the second trench and return to the first rapidly). The patiwale cannot leave their trench during an innings and can only move horizontally in the designated trench.
5. When the game starts, the first batch of four players from the lonawale team enter the field and start from the front trench. Then the second batch of the remaining four players and the trailer (the last player remaining after two batches) enter. The

trailer enters the court from the trench where the first player of the second batch was tagged out.

6. The lonawale players try to cross as many trenches as possible during the innings. They score one point for crossing each trench. The goal is to score a lona.
7. The lonawale players moving from the front trench to the last are known as up players, and the players returning from the last trench to the front are called down players. Lonawala players can move either to the right or the left half of the court while moving up and down.
8. The surr can't touch the lonawale without cutting the square. While the surr cuts the square, most of the players from the lonawale team reach the third trench.
9. At such a time, the surr obstructs the players by preventing them with the help of the third patiwala. It is known as making *kondi* (creating a ring/trap). Such a type of kondi can occur at any trench at any time.
10. There are various skills and tactics like dodging, pretending, falling and jumping to break the trap created by the patiwale. Some players try to reach lonapati while in the third trench.
11. The patiwale can hinder the lonawale by making a kondi and try to tag them out by touching them. Thus, if the team of lonawale is all out without getting lona, the patiwale now get an opportunity to play as lonawale.
12. A player who has crossed all the trenches is said to have achieved the lona.

After crossing all the trenches up to the last trench, when a lonawala reaches behind the last patiwala who is facing the front trench, he or she utters the word *tond* loudly and clearly, addressing the patiwala. Upon hearing this call, the patiwala immediately turns around and faces the back trench to obstruct the lonawala proceeding back towards the front trench. This action is called 'giving tond'. So the last patiwala now turns around and faces the direction for tagging the lonawala, which is now towards the front trench.

As soon as lona is scored by one player, that is, all the trenches are crossed, the referee announces the same. On such an announcement, all the lonawale who have not been tagged out must go to the front trench, and the game starts again. The duration of time for the innings is 7 minutes only.

Scoring

1. The team of lonawale scores one point for each trench crossed by every player while playing up or down, including the first trench. So when lona is achieved, the team scores 18 points in total, as each trench is crossed twice.
2. During the innings, if lona is left incomplete, the players get as many points as the number of trenches they have crossed. The team that scores more points and more lona in total after the three matches wins the game.
3. If there is a tie in a match, play continues for 60 seconds for each team with one batch of four

players. The team that scores more points in the given period is declared the winner.

Rules

1. If the surr does not cut the squares correctly, she gets the chance to cut the squares again but loses the chance after the surr crosses the third trench.
2. The surr, while tagging a patiwala out, can extend her foot within the lines of the trench, go up and down and change the direction as needed. Only hand touch is allowed as a form of tagging, and the surr can tag the left-side lonawale only with the left hand and the right-side players with the right hand.
3. Lonawala players can move through the right and left half of the court while proceeding up and down but cannot go reverse once the trench is crossed.
4. Fouling
    a. If an up player crosses a trench without a down player obtaining tond, the down player has committed a foul.
    b. If a down player, while going down, crosses a trench without obtaining tond, the down player has committed a foul.
    c. If any player goes out of the boundary or the patiwale players leave their assigned trench, a foul has been committed
5. The lonawala in the ring (three players in the same court) must have both their feet entirely within the boundaries of the ring and sidelines. They must not

go out of the lines while crossing the central trench, the trenches of the ring and the previous trench.

6. Lonawala cannot be tagged when they are just standing or passing the line or pretending to cross. Tagging is only allowed when a player actually passes the line.
7. When lonawala players have completely crossed a trench, they will not enter the court of the trench that has already been crossed.
8. A patiwala and the surr can both tag lonawale out from either side of the trench (right or left) while they are trying to cross the trench, whether they are an up player or a down player. But the patiwala *cannot tag opponents* if they have gone into the back trench; they cannot turn back and tag the lonawala in the front.
9. The lonawale players cannot step on any of the trench lines or run alongside another passing player.
10. A player who has scored a lona and another active lonawala player cannot stay in the same rectangle.
11. A patiwala cannot fall and tag, fall after tagging or touch the ground with their hands after successful tagging.
12. If patiwale step out of their line of defence, they cannot tag any lonawala.
13. If a match is not completed for any reason, it will be continued further on another occasion, and the scores of completed innings of each team will be counted.
14. Any loss in time during the game will be compensated. If the game is tied, 5 minutes is given to each team to play as lonawala, as a tiebreaker.

Positions, tasks and techniques

TABLE 14.2

Roles	*Positions*	*Tasks*	*Strategy / Techniques*
Lonawale	At the start, the first batch of four players stands just near the front trench.	Cross all the nine trenches and come back to the front trench without getting tagged out by the patiwale minding each rectangular court. After reaching the last trench, support the other proceeding teammates by asking for tond.	Move quickly and dodge constantly to break the concentration and divert the attention of the patiwala who is in front. Simultaneously, keep an eye on other teammates to support them by giving hints for safe and timely movements.
Patiwale	Stand in the vertical central trench, one on each square of the intersection. In the beginning, face the front trench, and after the tond, face the back trench.	Obstruct the proceeding lonawale and tag them out by touching with the hand while moving only in the designated horizontal track.	Be extremely vigilant and alert to check the directions and moves of the opponents. Form a ring with the support of the surr to trap the opponents and rule them out.

Roles	*Positions*	*Tasks*	*Strategy | Techniques*
Surr (captain)	Take a position in the front trench, ready to start the game by cutting the squares.	Start the game by cutting the first two trenches quickly while a batch of four lonawale enters the court. Obstruct their forward moves and tag them out while they move from one court to the next.	Be watchful and find out where to form a ring with the other patiwala to catch three or more proceeding lonawala players in the same court.

Key skills required

This game requires quick reflexes, strategic thinking, agility and alertness. It includes obstructing, dodging and tagging activities and, hence, is sometimes described as 'the game of feints'. For the best performance overall, physiological fitness plays a crucial role. Variables such as agility, reaction time, vital capacity and muscular endurance capacity of individuals can be additional qualities for the players.

The game requires a relatively small playing area and can also be played on the streets. Almost no equipment is needed, and it is easy to organise quickly. Age or gender is no constraint, but the player should be energetic enough for the necessary physical exertion. In the villages, the open fields are great for this game as injuries due to accidental falls can be minimised.

Cautions

The players should not push or obstruct the opponents by foot to try to aggressively tag them. This game is all about running fast and progressing despite hindrances. So each player should be cautious about balancing the body well to avoid stumbling.

Use hydrated lime powder or deeply engraved lines to mark the boundary and all the trenches because the frequent moves of the players may soon erase the lines marked by chalk.

Skills developed

Playing this game helps the body to be sturdy and healthy. Strenuous efforts develop physical, mental and neuromuscular coordination. In each trench, players need to stretch their bodies, which helps with fitness.

Life lessons

1. Even if one or more lonawale succeed in reaching the final stage, the game is not finished. The successful player is expected to retrace the way he or she crossed. The lonawala uses the benefits with which he or she is now qualified to lead and support others to achieve the same level.
2. Moreover, atya-patya is said to have spiritual references. The cross-section lines are obstacles that represent negative emotions like pride, ego, greed, anger, jealousy, hatred and so on, which

the progressive player on the spiritual path has to overcome. Only then can one get the divine qualities that are the spiritual goal.

Origin and references

This game was popular during the 16th century, and it is mentioned in the *abhangas* (verses) of the Marathi guru Shiromani Sant Tukaram Maharaj.

Traditionally, there were no approved rules for this game. Akhil Maharashtra Sharirik Shikshan Mandal made efforts to develop this game. They introduced the modern form of this game in 1935, along with the rules used even today.

Atya-patya Federation of India was formed in 1982, and the game was revived with the first national tournament held in Nagpur, India, in 1982.

Current state

For the first time, the National Atya-patya Championship was conducted in 2010 in Thane, India. Around 18 men's teams and 13 women's teams from around 24 states participated.

The first South Asian Atya-patya Championship was held in Bhutan in June 2013. It was won by India.

Variations of the game

In case of fewer players and a small playing area, you may reduce the number of trenches to 6 and the number of players to 12 in total. The playing method and rules would be the same as the main game.

Similar games

Surr

Surr is played between two teams, with a minimum of four players in each team, on a square court divided into four equal quadrants. Two perpendicular lines of defence run through the middle of the court, intersecting each other. The offence team gathers in the first quadrant while the defence players are on the lines of intersection.

The defence team's objective is to enter the other three quadrants without being touched by any defender. The defenders aim to stop them from doing so by tagging them. Any offence player who gets touched by a defender is ruled out of the game. The surviving offence players have to enter each quadrant one at a time and then gather in the square selected by defenders before entering the next square.

Once all the surviving offence team players gather in a new square, they shout '*bol den goivan surr!*' together.

If any offence player survives and reaches the final square, then their team wins the game. Otherwise, the defenders win.

Glossary

squares of intersection	Each of the small squares formed by the intersection of the central trench and the other trenches
court of a trench	Field between two adjacent trenches
patiwale	Those who stand on the trenches and hold them
surr	The patiwala who holds/defends the first and the central trench
lona	When any player from the lonawale team reaches the end and returns to the front trench, lona (finish the course) is scored against the patiwale
lonawale	The team on offence
trailer	Last player in the lonawale team
hand and foot fault	If any part of the feet of a patiwala or a surr touches the ground outside the lines of their respective trench, either in front or behind the player, they have committed a foot fault
cutting the squares	Going from the intersection of the first trench to the third trench and returning
tagging out	If a defender or a grenadier touches a lonawala by hand without breaching any rules, the lonawala is said to be tagged out

kondi/ring	When a patiwala and the surr enclose two or more lonawala in a square, it is known as a kondi or ring

15

Kabaddi

हुतुतू

भवतिक

કબડ્ડી

சடுகுடு

वैंडी

Introduction

Kabaddi is the most popular of the games in this book. It has also been recently revived for entertainment by the formation of professional leagues. In addition to being a popular game in India, it is also played in Iran, Bangladesh, Nepal and Pakistan. The game is derived from group hunting and village defence tactics. The word kabaddi has its origin in the Tamil phrase *kai pidi*, which means to hold hands. Rulers from Tamil Nadu spread this game to Southeast Asia during their sea trade.

In this contact sport, one player charges into the opponents' court and attempts to tag the nearby opponents, while all the other opponents manoeuvre to catch the raider.

Other names

TABLE 15.1

Region	*Name*	*Region*	*Name*
Andhra Pradesh	*Chedugudu saigudu*	Tamil Nadu	*Gudugudu, palinjadugudu, sadugudatthi*
Karnataka, Gujarat	*Kabaddi*	Thailand	*Thee-chub*
Kerala, Telangana	*Hududu*	Maldives	*Baibalaa*
Punjab	*Kaudi, hututu*	Bangladesh	*Bhavatik*
East India	*Chadukudu*	Nepal	*Dodo*
Northern India	*Kaun-bada*	Malaysia	*Chitgodo*

The play

The game's objective is for a raider to go to the opponents' court and attempt to touch one or more of the defenders without being caught by the defenders. Raiders have to recite kabaddi-kabaddi repeatedly and continuously till their breath runs out. The defenders have to constantly evaluate the raider's movements and find an opportunity to prevent the raiders from returning. The defenders need to have instant coordination.

Number of players

There are two teams, each consisting of seven active players and three additional players as substitutes.

Key officials

For formal games, the key officials are one referee, two umpires, one scorekeeper and two assistant scorekeepers. Informal games can be played with one person performing a combined role.

Duration of official matches

The game duration is 40 minutes with a change in sides after 20 minutes at half-time. There is a 5-minute break during the half-time when the teams switch sides.

A shorter period of 30 minutes is often considered for women, junior girls, sub-junior boys and sub-junior girls.

Equipment needed

Kabaddi does not need any special equipment for the play. Hydrated lime powder is needed to mark the boundaries.

The playground

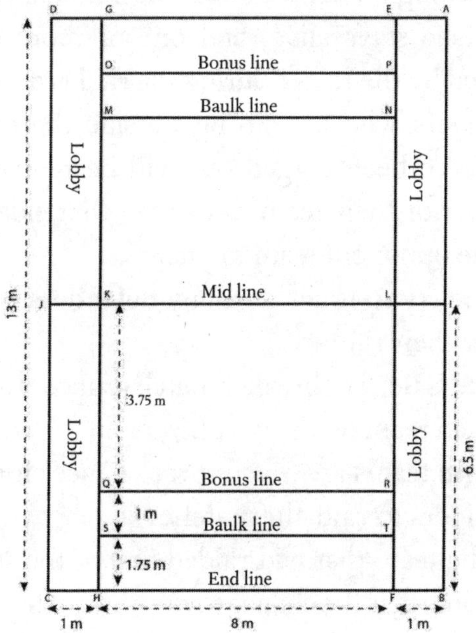

FIG 15.1. The kabaddi playground

The playing method

1. The team that wins the toss has the choice to take the role of raiders or defenders.
2. One of the raiders charges into the defender's boundary to tag any of the defenders. This move is called a 'raid'. The defenders must catch the raider and prevent him or her from returning to the raider's court. This is usually done by wrestling the raider to the ground till he or she loses breath.
3. If the raider is contained inside the defender's court, then the raider is out, and the defenders get a point.

4. If the raider succeeds in escaping the defender's hold, by touching the centreline or the boundary line, then he or she stays alive, and one or more defenders touched by the raider during the raid is declared out.
5. Defenders who are sitting outside the court after they have been tagged out will be revived once a member of their team raids the other side and tags out the opponent team members.
6. Raiders try to touch as many defenders as they can during their raid.
7. If there is tie, a tiebreaker match is played as follows:
   a. Each team fields five players on the court.
   b. Both teams are given three chances for different raiders to raid alternately.
   c. The team that had raided first at the start of the match gets the chance to raid first in the tiebreaker.

Rules

1. The raiders wait inside their designated court for their turn to raid. If any players come out of this area during the raid, then the raid is declared over. The defenders earn one technical point.
2. The raid continues till the raiders can hold their breath by reciting the word kabaddi repeatedly and continuously. If the raiders stay in the defenders' area and lose breath, then the defenders get one point.
3. No raider can take two consecutive raids. There must be a gap of at least one raid between two raids of the same raider.

4. Application of any greasy or oil-based substance on the body or limbs is not allowed.
5. Players who are out are revived once the raiders or the defenders succeed in tagging out one or more opponents.
6. A raider is declared safe if a defender touches the boundary line while holding the raider. Raiders get one point for each defender who has crossed the boundary while preventing the raider from returning.
7. If any player crosses the boundary line, the opposing team gets one point for each instance of crossing.
8. A team should send their raider within 10 seconds after the opposing team completes their raid. Thus, each side sends their raider alternatively until the end of the game.
9. A violent attack to hurt a raider is a foul. The attacker may be suspended, and the raiders get one point.
10. The teams switch their courts at half-time, and the total number of raids must be equal for both the teams in each innings.

Scoring

1. *Touch point*: Raiders get one point for each opponent they touch before returning successfully.
2. *Tackle point*: If the raider tries to touch a defender but is stopped by the defenders and cannot cross the midline, the defender team earns a tackle point.
3. Defenders get one point if they catch and hold the raider inside their area before the breath runs out.

Positions, tasks and techniques

Two sets of fundamental techniques are involved in the game.

1. *Raiding techniques*: These techniques are used by the raiders to touch the opponents and return safely.
    a. *Leading foot raid, turning hand touch*: Great acceleration and stretching is required from the raider to touch defenders before they have a chance to react and to get back home equally fast to avoid being tackled.
    b. *Toe touch*: Toe touch involves the raider ducking low to escape the defender's hands and attacking using feet to touch the defender. This is one of the most effective surprise attacks.
    c. *Side kick*: Touch the opponent with a side kick.
    d. *Scorpion kick*: The raider turns away from the defenders to face the midline. The raider curls his or her leg up backwards to touch the crouching defender, like a scorpion's sting. In addition to speed, this move requires balance, flexibility and surprise.
    e. *Front kick*: The raider kicks from the front in a swift and deceiving action.
    f. *Mule kick*: It is a deceiving kick where the raider quickly turns their back and kicks to quickly touch the defenders.
    g. *Frog jump*: Raiders launch themselves above incoming defenders and, while in the air, use their hands to propel themselves off the

defenders towards safety, thus tagging out the opponents.

2. *Defensive techniques*: These defensive techniques are used by the defenders to seize the raiders.
   a. *Knee catch*: In this, the defender grabs the raider's knee to restrict his or her movement towards the midline.
   b. *Ankle catch*: A defender catches the raider's ankle and pulls him or her away from the midline, making the raider fall.
   c. *Thigh catch*: The defender holds the raider's thighs, either a single thigh or both thighs.
   d. *Crocodile catch*: The defender holds the raider's arm from a distance first and then pulls it closer.
   e. *Wrist catch*: The defender grabs the raider's wrist and pulls him or her away from the midline.

Variations of the game

1. Variation in any or all the following areas are permissible: size of the playfield, the duration of play, weight and height of the players and substitutions.
2. Additional rules may be framed to make the game more strategic. For example, if a team has two empty raids in a row, the next raider must score a point on their next raid or else they will be out. This is called a do-or-die raid.
3. Additionally, when a defending team has less than four players left on the field, tackles are worth two points (super tackle).

Forms of kabaddi

In different parts of India, various forms of this game evolved, and today's kabaddi is a synthesis of these variations. In India, four types of kabaddis are played, as described next.

Amar

Amar means undying. In this form of kabaddi, whenever any player is tagged, he or she is not eliminated but stays in the court, and the play goes on. For every player tagged, the opposing team earns a point. This game is also played for a fixed time duration. This Amar form of kabaddi is also used by the World Kabaddi Federation (WKF) in its national, beach and circle kabaddi competitions.

Sanjeevani

In this form, one player is revived against one player of the opposing team who is out: one out, one in. This form of kabaddi is the closest to the present game. The team that eliminates all the opponent's sides gets four extra points.

Gaminee or gemini

In this format, an eliminated player stays out permanently. After all the players are tagged out, the team is revived, and the next round continues with all the players included. This format has no fixed time.

The disadvantage is that players get no chance to redeem themselves or perform better as they are out till everyone is eliminated.

Punjabi kabaddi or circle kabaddi

Punjabi kabaddi or circle-style kabaddi, which originated in the Punjab region, is also known as *dayare wali* kabaddi, meaning played inside a physical demarcation. This form is followed in major international tournaments like the Kabaddi World Cup and the World Kabaddi League.

The raider does not recite kabaddi during the raid, and there is a time of 30 seconds for each raid.

Key skills required

Kabaddi requires and develops physical strength and agility in young men and women. During its inception, it was played to boost self-defence skills and develop quick responsiveness to attacks. There are no restrictions on age, gender or weight to play. However, it would be good to have all the players of similar attributes to allow a balanced and enjoyable game.

Cautions

To eliminate the threat of causing abrasions, nails must be clipped, and players are not allowed to wear any accessories. Players with long hair should tie or clip the hair to prevent it from getting caught. Kabaddi is a physical game. Therefore, all players must restrict their moves to the legally allowed and safe moves.

Skills developed

Playing kabaddi develops agility, good muscular coordination, presence of mind, daring, quick reflexes, good lung capacity and an ability to anticipate the opponent's moves. The players learn to think logically and strategically improve their cognitive skills.

Life lessons

The game inculcates the right spirit to combat with opponents. The participants learn to defend themselves and their team members as well as to fight for them.

Kabaddi requires the team to plan a strategy, think logically and act accordingly. The play also involves running, kicking and dodging past the opponents. It requires one to move and think at the same time and very quickly. Impromptu team configurations and cooperation help develop such skills in real life as well.

Current state

Kabaddi was first introduced during the 1936 Berlin Olympics, where it was demonstrated by the Shree Hanuman Vyayam Prasarak Mandal from Amravati in

Maharashtra. The same group introduced Kabaddi in the Indian Olympic Games at Calcutta, India, in 1938.

In 1950, the All-India Kabaddi Federation was founded and compiled, and standard rules were structured. The Amateur Kabaddi Federation of India (AKFI) was founded in 1972, affiliated with the Indian Olympic Association (IOA), to spread the game in Asian countries. After the formation of the AKFI, the first men's national games were held in Chennai. India won the Kabaddi World Cup in 2007, beating Iran.

Kabaddi was included as a category in the 11th Asian Games in 1990. India won the gold medal in all the seven Asian Games except in 2018 when Iran won.

India is also the host to the world's first kabaddi league.

Origin

Kabaddi was popular in ancient India. An abhanga (a part of a poem) by Tukaram, a famous 17th-century Hindu saint, mentions that Krishna played kabaddi when he was young. Meanwhile, in the Mahabharata, Arjuna was able to intrude into the enemy labyrinth and kill enemies without being touched. Some relate this to the strategies of kabaddi.

Similar games

Dhopkhel is similar to Kabaddi and is played popularly in the Assam region. *Dhop* is a rubber ball that two teams throw across a central line into each other's courts. Each team sends a player into the opponent's court. The players in the opponent's court must catch the ball thrown by their team and make their way back to their team without allowing the opponents to touch them to earn points.

Glossary

mid line	Line that divides the playfield into two halves
court	Each half of the playfield, divided by the mid line
raider	One who enters the court of the opponent
defender	Every player in whose court the raid is being made
to put out a defender	If a raider touches any defender and then returns to his or her court, then the defender is said to be put out
to hold a raider	Defenders hold the raider and keep him or her in their court until the raider loses breath
to reach court safely	After the raid, If the raider touches the mid line with any part of the body without losing breath
raid	Charging into the opponent's court to tag them out

all out	When all the players of a team are ruled out of play, an all-out rule is implemented, and the raiding team earns four extra points for the same
self out	If any player goes out or is pushed out of the boundary line while raiding or defending, the opponents get one point

16

Pacha Kuthirai

பச்சை குதிரை

અંગકૂદકો

Luksong tinik
Thorn jump
Jump over me

Introduction

Players of *pacha kuthirai* jump over the hurdle created by the other players linking their hands and feet on the ground. The players must jump over the hurdle without touching the web of hands and feet. Two players position themselves on the ground to form the hurdle, and the remaining players jump over it in turns. The difficulty level of the hurdle increases when the stack is moved higher after every successful jump till the player fails to cross it.

Other names

TABLE 16.1

Region	*Name*		*Region*	*Name*
Punjab	*Adhi chharhapa*		Tamil Nadu	*Pacha kuthirai*
Gujarat	*Ang kudako*		Recently added in India	Thorn jump
Philippines	*Luksong tinik*		Western/English countries	Jump over me

The play

Number of players

Any number of players can join this game. One of the players is selected as a referee, though not needed for casual games as players govern themselves.

Equipment needed

No equipment is needed except white powder or a chalk stick to draw crease lines.

Playground

FIG. 16.1. A simple configuration

The game requires a relatively small area around 10 m long and 3 m wide. However, no boundary marking is needed. The flat surface area of any ground, street or school compound with grass can be the playfield. Gardens, parks and sandy land are preferred to avoid injury in the case of a fall during the play.

FIG. 16.2. A more complex configuration

Playing method

1. Pick any two players randomly to form a stack (the hurdle to jump over). Alternatively, to pick the sitting players, all the players take turns to jump, and the players who reach the shortest heights will be the sitting players.
2. These two players form the base of the hurdle. They sit on the ground in front of each other and extend their right feet and join their soles against each other.
3. The other players form a queue—about 2 m away from the two sitting players—to jump one by one.

Players line up in the increasing order of their age or height.

4. The game starts when the first player jumps over the stacked foot, one each, of the players on the ground. The player then returns and stands at the end of the line. The seated players keep adding one palm over both their feet to increase the stack's height after each gradual stage. This round of hurdle comprising five levels is complete when four hands on top of two feet are stacked.
5. If a player touches any part of the hands or the body of the sitting players while jumping, they are ruled out and take the place of one of the sitting players. The next time any player is ruled out, he or she takes the second place in the group of seated players and so on.
6. After five levels in the first round, the hurdle will be changed. One player forms a new hurdle by kneeling with both hands and knees touching the ground. The next level—sixth—will be a crouching position sitting with bending knees. The other sitting player would leave the hurdle formation.
7. The players gradually stand up as the game progresses, making it harder for the other players to jump over them. The seventh stage is bending from the waist and touching the hands on the ground near the feet, like a mountain.
8. In the final stage—eighth—of the hurdle, the crouching player is now standing straight but bending the head down. Other players jump over

this player without touching him or her. This is the most difficult high jump.

9. One can begin the game from a more challenging level by skipping some of the primary hurdles.

Rules

1. Each player gets only one chance to jump over the hurdle.
2. The jumping players must not touch the sitting players.
3. After a successful jump, each player must stand in the line to jump next.

Scoring

The winner is decided according to the difficulty level the players cross. The one who jumps the highest level is the winner, and then the other players are ranked.

Positions, tasks and techniques

TABLE 16.2

Roles	*Positions*	*Tasks*	*Strategy | Techniques*
Sitting players	Sit opposite the other sitting player to form the hurdle.	Sit comfortably, keeping adequate distance from the other sitting player.	Keep the configuration steady.

Roles	*Positions*	*Tasks*	*Strategy | Techniques*
Player on the move	Take a position on one side of the sitting players, about 2 m away from them.	Jump over the hurdle stack created by the two sitting players, and cross to the other side without touching them. Successively achieve the harder level in every turn.	Build an adequate speed before jumping to get the maximum height. For successive higher jumps, bend the knees while in the air to avoid touching the sitting players.
Other players	Line up behind the first player to get their turn to jump.	Observe each performance and wait for their turn to jump over. After every turn, join the queue again for the next level.	While observing, notice the style of every jump and learn the tactics from the previous players' jumps to improve own performance at the next level.

Key skills required

Pacha kuthirai requires free mobility and stretching, so the ability of the players to move easily and freely is essential. Lower body flexibility and a wide range of motor movements play a crucial role.

An additional skill is keeping the body parts steady, especially the waist. Once players are stable, they can jump higher. The game is enjoyable primarily for children and teenagers aged six to sixteen, though age or gender is not a restriction for those who like high jumps. Tall players have an advantage because high jumps are essential for winning.

Caution

The active players must be careful not to hurt or push the sitting players. They must first assess their capability at lower levels before moving to higher levels.

Variation

One can set more than one hurdle in a series at a fixed distance to cross them in one go.

To help beginners, one can set flexible rules, for example, allowing the jumping players to take support by putting their hands on the backs of the sitting players.

Skills developed

This street game enhances jumping ability and body flexibility, and provides training for some yoga postures.

Life lessons

In this game, players allow others to jump over them. This concept inculcates cooperative and supportive nature in children as they become an instrument for the progress of others and get the same help from others when they play.

Current state

This simple game with basic physical exercise has almost vanished from the playgrounds. Until the 1980s, it was popular in villages and small towns.

Similar games

Luksong baka is a traditional Filipino high jump game that originated in Bulacan, Philippines. Players jump over a person called the *baka* (cow), who bends to form a hurdle. The main difference is that players can support themselves by putting their hands on the back of the baka while jumping.

Glossary

pacha kuthirai	Green horse

17

Worthy Mentions

While we described 15 games in detail, we picked a few other games to mention in brief. These popular games are also simple to organise and play.

Dhopkhel

Dhopkhel is a traditional ball game played in Assam as a part of welcoming spring and celebrating the new year festival of Bihu. Players throw a ball from a distance to tag out opponents. So they need to judge the direction and force of the throw. It requires swiftness and acrobatic agility.

Two teams of 11 members each play this game on a 125 m x 80 m field bounded by four red flags. Players throw the ball at the opposing team members to tag them out, while the opposing team seeks to catch the ball and throw it back to the first team. The objective is the same, to tag one of the players. Tagging players standing near a corner is easier as they do not have much open space to run to.

The player who is tagged out has to go to the opponent's side and prevent the opponent's team from catching the ball thrown by his or her native team.

That player catches the ball and brings it back to the native team without being touched by the opponents. There would be multiple players from both teams on both sides on the court. The game is a test of speed, strength and motor skills.

Kati

Pioneered by the Santhal and Bhumij tribal communities, Kati is traditionally played as a summer pastime after the harvest season. It is played between two teams of nine players each. Each player has a kati, a half-moon-shaped disc usually made from the wood of the tamarind tree as it is lighter in weight, and a *tarhi*, a 6 ft to 7 ft long bamboo rod. The game involves strenuous footwork, sharp observation and quick limber moves.

Players must hit the kati with a tarhi to strike the opponent's kati. The striking team lines up on the boundary with their kati and tarhi. The defender's kati are placed in a row on the midline of the rectangular field. The objective of the striking team player is to send their kati to the defender's court but after striking the opponent's kati that is placed midway. Strikers propel the bamboo stick with the foot to hit their own kati to strike it with the opponent's kati.

Every successful strike earns a point. Each time they displace the kati with their stick, players earn a point. Watch the exciting gameplay here.[1]

1 https://www.youtube.com/watch?v=e9nMP3oiJ_E

Sagol kangjei

It is said that the game of sagol kangjei started during the reign of Kangba, who is considered the first king of Manipur. *Kangjei* means Kangba's stick, and *sagol* means a horse. Sagol kangjei literally means hockey on horseback. Kangba is a round object like a ball, and *jei* is the stick for hitting the object. This ancient game is also called the mother of modern polo.

Two teams with seven players each play the game, and each player is equipped with a jei, a wooden stick, 4 ft to 5 ft long, made of cane wood. A long piece of wood, about 1 ft, is fixed at one end to form a T-shape. Players strike the ball with the T-shaped end. The ball is about 3 in in diameter, made of bamboo roots. The players ride horses/ponies to play and hit the ball out of the goal boundary. Watch a video here.[2]

Noon miani

Noon miani is very popular in the Punjab region. With the basic objective of grabbing something and escaping, the game involves running and chasing in bounded tracks.

Four boxes of equal size, measuring 25 m x 25 m, are drawn on the ground, leaving a 2 m track between two adjacent boxes and 2 m on the outer boundary of all boxes.

[2] https://www.youtube.com/watch?v=i7sspeH_uec

In the centre of the four boxes, a fifth square is drawn and filled with salt or sand. The key player minds the salt or sand, standing in the same square. Outside the boundary, usually to the north, a rectangle is drawn, called a *sandook*. Other players try to steal the salt and rush out of the boundary through the tracks towards the sandook. The key player's objective is to catch the players who try to get the salt while moving in the bounded tracks.

Pambaram | Lattu| Tuoluo | Tops

Traditionally, tops were constructed of wood, sometimes with an iron tip at the bottom. The game of spinning has dozens of variations, and many can be improvised by the players. Some play the spinning top on their palm; some make it a group game and compete for the period of time a player's top can spin before falling.

The top is set in motion using a string or rope coiled around its axis that causes a rapid unwinding when pulled quickly. The rope unwinds itself as the top rotates by the friction between the top and the rope. Harder the pull keeping the equilibrium, the longer the spin. Advanced players also include movements on the surface as the top spins.

Bandar kila (Bandar khoonti)

A popular game said to have originated in the villages of Punjab, bandar kila is a simple street game. The game involves the fun activities of teasing, escaping and stealing chappals from the selected player's area.

At the start of the game, one player (bandar) is tied to a pole (kila), and all the other players place their chappals or shoes near that pole. The bandar has to protect those shoes from all the players. During this competition, the bandar tries to touch other players when they come close to the pole to steal the chappals. The player who is caught becomes the bandar for the next round, and the game continues. Watch the video here.[3]

Gutte

This game is also called *kuzhangal* or *anchankal* in the villages of Tamil Nadu. In Malaysia, it is known as *batu seremban* and *selambut*. A variant of gutte is known as jackstones or knucklebones in Western countries. This game is popularly played by children in groups of two or more. It is often played at leisure on any clean flat surface. Five stones of similar size are used for the game. (Small triangular cloth bags filled with seeds, rice or sand also can be used as substitutes for the stones.)

The game involves throwing the stones up in the air and catching them as they fall. It is played in various sequential and predetermined levels. One stone is tossed up in the air at a time, and one or more are picked up from the ground while the tossed stone is in the air. The game continues to eight levels, where the number of

[3] https://www.youtube.com/watch?v=vNv69sutE3A

stones picked up increases in each throw. The objective is to complete a set of eight steps.

Watch the game on YouTube.[4]

Vandi vruttuthal (Hoop rolling | Krikoi | Trochus)

In vandi vruttuthal, a large hoop is rolled along the ground, struck and pushed by a stick to keep it moving.

Hoops were earlier made of metal such as bronze, iron or copper and were driven with a stick. The hoop is sized according to the height of the player, made to be just below chest height. The long handle can be rolled by a small stick or bamboo whip about 1 m long. Another way to play is to push the hoop with a U-shaped iron hook.

Children would be surprised to find that the iron ring at the bottom of an abandoned iron drum can also be used as a hoop. These iron drums are discarded after they develop holes and can't hold grains anymore. Players can make the hoop go straight and turn. They can also use an iron hook to smash the bottom of the iron ring and let the iron ring return or make the iron ring jump without falling.

One can use a discarded bicycle rim or a tyre to roll.[5] More skill is needed than it may appear to. While not typically considered a game in itself, this sport is physically exerting and focused on a central goal: to keep the hoop rolling as long as possible. A group can compete on the basis of speed of running

[4] https://www.youtube.com/watch?v=V70PoydBCck

[5] https://www.youtube.com/watch?v=BfXelQxW80A

with the hoop—fastest and slowest, and several other configurations.

Chaki badi | Chaki khela

Chaki badi is one of the oldest games in parts of Odisha, popular among the Juang tribe. It is played by hitting a *chaki* (circular shape, cut from used slippers) with a wooden stick called the *chakibadi*. Watch it on YouTube.[6]

It is a fun game where players (usually comprising both children and adults) are divided into two teams of seven to nine players each. The matches are played in a rectangular field measuring about 100 sq ft with the boundary demarcated by bamboo sticks at the four corners, similar to a football field.

Goti | Marbles

Bright, spherical and colourful glass/stone marbles have attracted children for ages. There are a variety of games played using this prop. Generally, little marbles, 1 cm to 2.5 cm in diameter and made of sand, lime and soda ash, are used for playing.

One popular version involves aiming at any one marble amongst many that are placed in a circle, one by each player. The players roll their master marble with the jerk of a finger to hit the target marble from a fixed distance of about 3 ft. If the targeted marble rolls out from the circle, the player gains that marble.

[6] https://www.youtube.com/watch?v=U8yEVxflxq4

Another variation involves sending a marble into a hole dug in the ground. Each player has to roll his or her marble from a distance of about 12 ft and with exact force to send it into the targeted hole. We may relate this to *putting* in the game of golf.

Mukna kangjei (Manipur hockey)

Mukna kangjei, also known as *khong* kangjei and commonly known as Manipuri hockey, is played with cane sticks. The game is a very rare and unique combination of kangjei (hockey) and mukna (a form of Manipuri wrestling). It requires stamina, speed and agility, which reflects the martial tradition of Manipur.

The game is played by two teams of seven players each. In the game, players hit the ball with their sticks and wrestle with each other to win the ball. They prevent each other from striking the ball by holding the opponents back or pushing them down to the ground, just like in wrestling. There is no goalpost, but a goal is scored when the ball crosses the goal line. Watch the game on YouTube.[7]

Lathi chor (A stick thief)

Traditionally, tree-climbing games were favourite vacation activities in India. One of the games popular in West Bengal was *lathi chor* (stick thief). Five or six players gather near a tree. A circle of 2 ft diameter is

[7] https://www.youtube.com/watch?v=g1LksDHJwg4

drawn to place a small stick into it. One of the players picks up the stick and throws it with maximum force, swinging it from under his or her leg.

The player selected to be the chaser runs towards the stick and brings it back. Meanwhile, all the other players climb up the tree quickly and jump down to pick the stick from the circle. The chaser tries to catch them when they come near the circle. Whoever is caught while picking up the stick from the ground will be declared out and becomes the chaser in the next round of the game.

Sekkor

Sekkor is a 10-in-long cylindrical wooden object with a diameter of about 8 in at the centre and 3 in at the narrow edges. It is hand-carved to allow rotation on its axis from one edge. The Ho tribals of the Chaibasa area of Jharkhand play this game.

The game is played between 2 teams of 5 to 11 players in each team on a ground 30 ft long and 27 ft wide. In the middle of the ground, four or five sekkors are placed in a small circle.

The competition is based on striking the sekkors placed in the centre of the ground with the master sekkor that is in the player's hands. The objective is to send the sekkors out of the boundary. A cotton rope of 10 ft is wrapped around the axis of the master sekkor to lift it up and throw it to collide with the targeted sekkors, like we lift and throw tops with a string. Here the thick, twisted cotton rope is tied and wrapped to the sekkor to send it far away with an unwinding of the rope. The team gets five points to hit the sekkor out of the boundary. The team player who sends it back in the ground also gets five points.

Watch the game on YouTube.[8]

Surr

Surr is a popular traditional game widely played in northern India, particularly in and around Ayodhya. The game involves a basic activity, though it is based on inflexible strict rules.

It is played on a square court divided into four equal quadrants by two intersecting tracks (lines of defence) that run through the middle of the court. These tracks are held by the defence team members.

The offence team assembles in one of the quadrants, which are called houses or rooms. The runners aim to enter the other three quadrants, but in doing so, they should not be touched by any of the defensive players who strive to prevent the runners. If they are touched, they are declared out and must step out of the game.

The other surviving offence team members must try to access every quadrant, and finally gather in any one of the quadrants selected by the defenders before proceeding to the next quadrant they suggest. As soon as all the players gather in the new quadrant, they joyfully shout, '*bol den goivan surr!*'

[8] https://www.youtube.com/watch?v=KofnvsswmHg

The offence team has to survive the touch of the defence members and finish the course of moving in all four quadrants in a given order.

18

Conclusion

Playing games is inherent to nature. Animals play all the time, and since humans have advanced faculties, the range of games possible is practically unlimited. Games naturally evolve based on the terrain and tools available. Each region in India too had its own set of games, but many disappeared over the past two centuries or so.

Historical references

Games have traditionally been a part of Indian physical well-being and entertainment, like any other region in the world. Indian social occasions and festivals also invited participation in various games as a part of the celebrations. The Sanskrit word *kreeda*[1] refers to 'games and recreational activities' and formed part of the Indian education system that aimed at growing both the inner and outer dimensions of a person. The vital component of kreeda is the delight one derives from voluntary participation in games along with the unity of nature and the environment. There are eight limbs of yoga (ashtanga), and three of them

[1] https://www.wisdomlib.org/definition/krida

focus on physical well-being—pranayam (balancing the breathing), pratyahar (refining the senses) and asan (strengthening the body). Most Indian games generally incorporate one or more of these three.

Physical strength, self-defence and combative arts have been the core aspects of a routine lifestyle. Ancient Indian texts such as Vedic literature, the Ramayana, the Mahabharata, and the Puranas mention numerous games and sports. Coins, dice, stone balls and marbles found in archaeological excavations and symbol carvings are evidence of an active sports culture.

> Who of men today has been adorned with so many petals and myrtles and crowns of rose, thanks to his victory in the games?
>
> —Simonides's Ode to Astylos

Unlike the common practice in many communities today, women too participated in sports, the same as men. The Rigveda mentions women joining the army, and the chariot race, which included women participants, was one of the popular sports during the Vedic era. Both men and women enjoyed swings and ball games, besides courtyard games like hide-and-seek and run-and-chase. Even today, there is little gender difference in games played in the villages.

Dhanurveda, one of the *Upvedas* of the Yajurveda, discusses the detailed battle strategies and fighting methods of the Vedic science of war. Arjun's mastery in archery (*Dhanurveda*), even while blindfolded, depicts the importance of combative arts.

Many games that the West has patented, such as Ludo, Parcheesi, and Snakes and Ladders, are of Indian origin and were popular with the names *chausar*, *pachisi* and *moksh pattam*. The Indian board game *chaturanga/ ashtapada* is sold as chess now.

Benefits of playing these games

Games are not just fun but also beneficial. In the hierarchy of needs, sports rank just after physical needs, such as food and shelter, because it provides multidimensional benefits including health, entertainment and social connections. While entertainment is expected to cost money, for example, watching movies or going to a resort, physical activities do not cost much normally unless one takes a gym membership. In any case, the games we have picked would not need expensive club memberships or gym subscriptions.

> You miss 100 percent of the shots you don't take.
>
> —Wayne Gretzky

Playing games is a great connector—it connects people across ages, religions, genders and socio-economic statuses. Playing our traditional games with family brings the family closer and strengthens the bond. Strong family relationships positively affect every aspect of life, even at later stages. The bonds made during childhood while playing games often stay for life. Most of us adults look back and fondly remember the people we played with in childhood. Nothing else can replicate such connections. Playing games creates memories—fond memories of childhood that we all relish even when we are older.

Enthusiasm and curiosity in kids need unstructured playtime—it makes them creative and helps develop special skills.

Games provide the following benefits:

1. Enhance physical well-being, reduce health challenges and improve the health of internal organs, leading to increased longevity
2. Add physical strength, agility, stamina and swiftness; build muscles; reduce fat; and develop mental agility and quick-decision making
3. Increase physical attractiveness, shape the body and improve posture
4. Heighten physical confidence leading to societal confidence
5. Develop motor skills and mind-body coordination
6. Provide empowerment and self-validation, and feed the ego, especially when winning against opponents
7. Provide motivation to achieve higher
8. Develop leadership, force the player to take the initiative and decide actions. The success of the team depends on the performance of each, leading to a sense of responsibility
9. Develop team spirit, coordination and sharing of risks and rewards

10. Develop a sense of observation and teaches obedience
11. Create social bonding. Teammates are often best friends for life. Many sportspersons find life partners from the sporting community
12. Promote psychological and physical development
13. Sharpen spontaneous cognitive training as sports need instantaneous responses
14. Teach players to respect rules and comply with them
15. Teach players to confront if another player violates rules or if processes are not honoured
16. Teach players to accept and honour decisions, for example, of a referee, even if there are disagreements. They learn to accept an unfair decision, as life presents several circumstances with unfair decisions
17. Teach life lessons of engaging with multiple people, without any power over them, and driving a decision. Players learn to build consensus

> How you respond to the challenge in the second half will determine what you become after the game, whether you are a winner or a loser.
>
> —Lou Holtz

Life lessons

Through games, players learn to:

1. use stress as motivation
2. perform under pressure
3. make mistakes while learning

4. manage the fear of losing and learn that life isn't always fair
5. focus on what they can control
6. accept defeat in a fair game and develop a positive attitude
7. respect the opponents
8. be accountable and responsible
9. acknowledge winning honourably
10. develop a killer instinct
11. not give up, and to chase goals and targets
12. think analytically
13. think and act swiftly
14. set and achieve goals
15. observe the strengths, weaknesses and mindsets of others
16. be disciplined, and
17. manage time effectively and efficiently

> One man practicing sportsmanship is far better than 50 preaching it.
>
> —Knute Rockne

Saving Indian games is saving Indian culture

> Due to colonisation and religious conversions, various regions from different continents lost their unique local heritage and appear indistinguishable from each other today.

We have lost our education system. Our education system, even in government schools, is modelled after British schools, where Indianness has been eliminated. Our languages are treated as second class and are not considered worthy of conducting business in. We have lost our attire. Indian clothes are not considered acceptable in offices or for entering a social club. Most of our indigenous grains are disappearing in favour of wheat. *Makka*, bajra, *jau*, *juvar*, *madua*/ ragi, *saama*, *kodo*, *rajgira*, *cheena* and *maarha* have vanished from my region. There were at least 15 types of fruits I ate growing up, but only mangoes, guavas and bananas have survived. Fruits like *mahua*, *jaamun*, *ghurmindi*, *kadamb*, *baer*, *misrikand*, *shakarkand* and *shahtoot* are all gone from my region. Even in villages, the fruits sold in the market are apples and oranges. Local farmers grow broccoli to feed the urban people, who, in turn, are influenced by the West. So the entire ecosystem is influenced by the West.

Our music industry does not use sitar, veena or dholak. We have moved to not only Western instruments like guitar and drums but also Western tunes. When a song starts, I normally think it is an English song till the singer utters Urdu words.

Our games also face the same fate. Rich urban Indians just follow the West. Sports means the ones played in the West at the Olympics. Poor urban Indians aspire to do what the urban rich do. Similarly, people from smaller towns look up to urban Indians. Villagers are out of the equation. Over time, a sense has developed that their life, culture and life is not up to the mark, and city folks are the people to take directions from.

Every country that was either colonised or attacked by intruders has lost its original culture, lifestyle as well as indigenous sports. British colonies play similar games, including India.

ततो ददर्शोपवने वरस्त्रियंविचित्रपुष्पारुणपल्लवद्रुमे । विक्रीडतीं कन्दकलीलया लसद्-दुकूलपर्यस्तनितम्बमेखलाम् ॥

> Sports must become an indispensable and inseparable part of our social life. Competitiveness is just a by-product.
>
> —Narendra Modi

This canto from the *Śrīmad-Bhāgavatam* says that Lord Siva saw a beautiful woman in an elegant attire playing a ball. The Mahabharata and the Puranas mention various ball (*kandukam*) games as childhood sports of Krishna and his contemporaries. Games like lagori have enthralled the people of India for five millennia.

Time to turn things around[2]

The idea for the book came about when Sangeeta asked Amitabh (both authors of this book) about his interest in sports. Amitabh plays squash, golf, badminton and tennis—all Western games. But growing up in a village, he played all the local games. Sangeeta played several games as a student, and when she founded an NGO, she had children play traditional games. It often

[2] https://vedabase.io/en/library/sb/8/12/18/

does not occur to us that the terms 'sports and games' have become synonymous with Western sports only. So the idea for this book took shape to help revive our ancient treasures that are struggling under the weight of Western hegemony.

Our country is going through a churn. After foreigners succeeded in convincing us that everything Indian is not good and anything foreign is good, some of us are rising and challenging that belief.

Our games are fun and interesting and can be played conveniently. They cost nothing or almost nothing to play, especially the games we have selected. Encouraging these games will allow the players to receive all the benefits mentioned earlier and will require almost no investment. The investment required in lakhs of crores of rupees for building thousands of tennis courts, cricket stadiums and swimming pools is not needed. Indian games give, say, a hundred times better return on investment. Investment in Western games does help win some medals in international competitions, such as the Olympics. However, if we wish to build character, develop team spirit and provide physical exercise, then Indian games are as good or better than the Western ones.

Expensive schools invest in developing Western sports facilities. They must consider creating space for Indian games or sharing space with a tennis or basketball court. A tennis court is good for only two players, whereas the same space can be used by dozens of players playing Indian games.

HAPPY PLAYING

ABOUT THE AUTHORS

Amitabh Satyam is a sports enthusiast who represented his college in gymnastics and athletics. A graduate of the Indian Institute of Technology Kanpur, India, with an MBA from Fisher College of Business, United States of America, he has held leadership roles at SAP, IBM, Siemens and Reliance Infocomm.

He grew up playing Indian games in his village and brings this experience to the book. He plays squash and golf today.

Sangeeta Goswami is a founder of the Sri Life Global Foundation. With a background in mathematics and education and a master's degree in psychology, she is a researcher of cognitive behaviour, and currently practises counselling psychology.

She taught sports in school in addition to mathematics. She is a coordinator at experimental methodology schools promoting integral education.